JonBenét Ramsey. The Great American tragedy.

By Alex Duggan.

Contents

Part One.

The Sense of an Ending.

Chapter 1

A Picture Perfect Family.

A system of cells interlinked, within cells interlinked, within cells interlinked within one stem. And dreadfully distinct against the dark, a tall white fountain played.

Vladimir Nabokov, *Pale Fire*.

If you wanted a picture of the American Dream, you only had to look at the Ramsey family in the summer of 1996. John Ramsey was born on the infamous date of December 7th, only this time in 1943. He joined the Navy after high school, serving his country in the Philippines. By the 1970's he was married with three children and working in the pioneering field of computers. In the 80's he got divorced. He also set up a computer marketing company called *Access Graphics*. He met his second wife, Patsy, and had two more children. By 1996 John was a millionaire. He had moved his family to a large house in Boulder, Colorado. In December of that year a local newspaper reported that his company had turned over a billion dollars in twelve months and was working closely with Lockheed Martin, one of the largest defence companies in the world.

Patsy Ramsey was born on December 29th, 1956. She was voted Miss West Virginia at the age of twenty. The beauty pageant queen was also highly intelligent, gaining a Bachelor of Arts degree in journalism from West Virginia University. She met John soon after. They married, and for the next few years Patsy helped John to get his company started. Both Patsy and John were devout Christians and attended the local Episcopal church. As a mother with two children she would often organise school fundraising events and used her southern charm when entertaining guests in their house just a few miles away from the Flat Irons Mountain range.

Burke Ramsey was born on 27th January 1987. He was quiet, like his father. He joined the Boy Scouts, possibly as a way of getting out more, spending the summer of 96 at a camp. But Burke was also part of the first generation being brought up on home computers. The family had spoken about all getting bikes that year, but what Burke really wanted for Christmas was the new *Nintendo 64*. His parents had relented and agreed, but for his birthday a month later he would be getting a new bike.

JonBenét, a fancy French version of her father's first and middle name, arrived in the world on August 6th, 1990, the only one in the family who wasn't born in the Winter. Like most girls she enjoyed dressing up, attending a local dance class, and by the fall of 1996 she had started Kindergarten. JonBenét was also involved in child beauty pageantries. These were shows where young girls would perform a song or a dance, parade in different outfits, and be judged as if in an adult beauty competition. You could argue that Tom Brady was attending football summer camps from the age of five, Britney Spears was performing in musical theatre around the same age, and Beyonce won her first singing competition at the age of seven. But these pageants seem to be more about wealth and the sexualisation of children than any real talent. And with people being able to create their own websites since 1994 and the rise of men possessing indecent images of children, the idea of a six-year-old girl wearing full make-up and dressed in provocative clothing would later become an issue that both John and Patsy would be judged on.

It seemed that Patsy was just as involved in these pageant competitions as JonBenét. It was Patsy who bought the expensive handmade dresses her daughter might only wear once, and it was Patsy who spent thousands of dollars making her daughter have professional photo sessions, dance classes, bleaching her hair blonde, and travelling together all over the country. Where Burke stayed during these weekends away I don't know.

December was going to be a busy month, with pageant shows, parties, holidays, and Patsy's fortieth birthday to arrange. They were planning to spend Christmas morning at home, then at their friend Fleet White's house in the evening, just like they did last Christmas. The next day would be a private plane flight to Michigan to spend some time with Johns older children, then fly back a few days later and take a commercial flight to Florida to spend time on a Disney Cruise ship for a few days before flying back to Colorado and Burke's birthday.

On Christmas morning the children opened their presents. John drove to the airport to put some presents on their plane. A few of the neighbourhood kids came over to play. There was a bit of a tantrum when JonBenét refused to wear the same clothes as Patsy to the party: black trousers and a red turtleneck top. Instead, JonBenét wore a white top. They went to Fleet White's house and chatted with other friends and their children. When they returned home later that night, the sleeping JonBenét was carried up to bed. The alarm was not turned on. Even though it was a large house, Boulder was a quiet sort of American town. There had not been one reported homicide that year. But the next morning the residents of Boulder woke to find the American dream had been destroyed.

When Patsy went down the stairs, she found a ransom note laid out on one of the bottom steps. A kidnapper had taken her daughter and they wanted money. Patsy called for up for John, then called the police. She also called some of her friends to come over and help. The ransom note said they would phone later that morning to swap the money for their daughter. Everyone waited. The call never came. After a few hours a detective asked John to search the house for anything that looked out of place. In a locked room in the basement John found his daughter's lifeless body. The kidnapping turned into a murder investigation on the afternoon of 26th December 1996. An investigation that continues to this day.

From the very beginning there have been two different versions of events running alongside each other. There are those who believed an intruder committed this crime, and those who believe someone in the house was involved. For many it's because the initial accounts from the family did not match the evidence. For others it's because the initial police investigation was incompetent at best, and biased against the Ramseys even though there is the evidence of the ransom note to support an intruder did it. But this doesn't really answer why JonBenét's death has remained unsolved after all this time.

Perhaps this is the reason why we are so fascinated by this tragedy. We like our fictional crime to have all the pieces fit into the final picture. In a novel such as Agatha Christie's *Murder on the Orient Express,* there is a narrative that starts by setting the scene and who the players are. The stage is set, the crime is committed, and clues are left behind for us to follow. We get to the last act and the killer is revealed. The motive is explained, the mystery is solved, justice is served. There may have been deception along the way, we may have wander down the wrong path at the start; but in the end justice is restored and our view of the universe returns to normal. With true crime, even when some of the pieces are missing, we still like to get to the end, and to believe that even though evil is always just below the surface there are still some things in this world worth fighting for.

The problem with the JonBenét Ramsey investigation having two theories and no final act is that the truth continually changes from one viewpoint to another, essentially making both narrators unreliable. There have been numerous books on the investigation, as well as TV programmes, films, Youtube videos and podcasts. They include allegations JonBenét had been sexually abused by a secret paedophile group, that the intruder was an evil psychopath, that John and Patsy spent millions of dollars on private investigators just to avoid prosecution, and the police had tried to charge an innocent person. There were also consistent rumours of a lack of integrity within the District Attorney's office in their failure to prosecute the Ramseys for the last thirty years, and stories about the police holding back DNA evidence which could find the intruder and solve the case. Sometimes it all feels more like entertainment than news. The fictional end of the American Dream coincided with the failure to find out who killed a six-year-old girl. How did this happen. How have we not solved this crime? Perhaps there is an answer.

Chapter 2

The American Dream was a Television Show.

And so, my fellow Americans: ask not what your country can do for you — ask what you can do for your country.

John F. Kennedy's Inaugural Address, January 20, 1961.

JonBenét missed out by eight months on being an eighties child. The decade of Ronald Reagan, MTV, the Cold War, and video cassettes was also the last act of the American Dream. Those watching those great historical events on television did not notice that everything around them was slowly being produced in a different country. Even the national flag they picked up to welcome in the nineties was being made in Taiwan. Cars, jeans, electronics and even their oil was being produced somewhere else. At least America could claim had won the war for democracy. President, George H. Bush watched as Russian and Chinese communism began to fall. The old dictatorships had killed around sixty million of their own people between them, and America had spent billions of dollars stopping their regimes from killing more. The world was now free to enter a new millennium in peace. But sometimes things gain a momentum of their own.

When Saddam Hussein invaded Kuwait, America stepped in to stop him. Oil may just be liquified dead DNA, but it fuelled the global economy. The fight was over quicker than Mike Tyson in his prime. What was barely noticeable in the news were reports by Saddam Hussein complaining that the Muslim world had let him down by siding with the white infidels. Political fanaticism was being replaced by religious ones. America, believing that race and religion had been consigned to the previous century, was in for a shock.

Bush expected to be re-elected, but a new man had arrived. Bill Clinton was the first president who had not served his country. Muhammad Ali got five years in jail for refusing to fight to Vietnamese. Clinton went to Oxford University in England and got a degree. Clinton won because he had a tough strong wife by his side, and he told the people he was going to lead America into the next millennium safer, richer, and more peaceful than it had ever been. The money spent on fighting injustice all over the world could now be spent bringing justice to the American people. The internet would give a person access to every library book in the world. Computers were going to change everything. For a businessman such as John Ramsey, he must have felt as though the whole universe was turning his life into a dream. No one ever suspects the cost must be paid in nightmares.

Born just a year after President Clinton, O. J. Simpson had a slightly different childhood. As a young man he was on the road to crime until someone noticed his running ability might be better suited on the football field. A star during the seventies, Simpson turned from football to acting in the eighties before marrying the blonde-haired Nicole Brown and having two children. Behind the smile for the cameras there was a darker side. Simpson assaulted Nicole on numerous occasions until they divorced in 1992. But Simpson didn't like losing at anything and continued to stalk his ex-wife for the next two years. One night in 1994 Nicole had left a pair of glasses in a restaurant, and the waiter Ron Goldman went to the house to drop them off. Both were brutally attacked and stabbed to death outside Nicole's front door. When police arrived, they found a glove left at the scene and some drops of blood they believed belonged to the killer. Detectives then went to Simpsons house to inform him of the tragedy. They noticed his car had bloodstains on it. Believing he could also be the victim of an assault they went into his house without a warrant, where they found a glove which matched the one left at the crime scene. Simpson had flown to Chicago just an hour before. Detectives left messages for Simpson to call them. When he finally did, he appeared to implicate himself in the murders by never bothering to ask how, where, or when his ex-wife had died. He was then allowed to wander around the country for a few days while his DNA was checked against DNA found at the crime scene. When he did arrive home, he handed an attaché case to his old friend Robert Kardashian and then asked him to be his lawyer. This meant he had client privilege and could never be asked about the case that quickly disappeared. When the DNA came back as a match, the police asked Simpson to come into the police station. He declined, and instead he kidnapped himself, alleging he was going to die as he drove around Los Angeles. Whether this was by the hands of the police or his own he never made clear. This self-abduction was shown on every television channel, with newspapers and magazines worldwide picking up the story.

Finally arrested, there was then another couple of weeks in which the defence argued Simpson would never receive a fair trial due to the publicity (he had created). While all this was going on, numerous witnesses were selling their stories for thousands of dollars. Later, these witnesses would have their evidence either not heard or dismissed due to defence arguing it had been tainted. Among the people in the spotlight was Simpsons friend and now lawyer Robert Kardashian. For Mr Kardashian's daughters, all this publicity seemed to make them popular.

By the time the trial started, the multi-millionaire Simpson has spent a fortune on a defence team whose morals and integrity some people thought were highly questionable, but there was a reason why they were getting paid more than the prosecution team, they were better at their job. And that job was getting their famous running back to walk out of court. They told the world that Simpson was arrested because of his genetic make-up. He had been presumed guilty by being black. And the theme of genetics kept coming up. Many Americans still believed that swearing on the Bible meant you had to tell the truth. The idea that a person's guilt or innocence might rely on DNA was pure fiction. They were to soon realise that a tiny cell among the many millions moving around your body could be the most powerful thing in the universe.

Television was still King in 1995, although the idea of America being represented by a white middle class family with two children was slowly changing. Eighties sitcoms such as *The Wonder Years* and *Family Ties* made way for *The Cosby Show* and *Friends*. And now there was an intruder in the house. Cable television. From specialist entertainment such as sport, there were also news channels.

They soon realised that people didn't want dry reports, the wanted the same sort of spectacle you find on the playing field. When the Twin Towers was bombed in 1993 it was the first foreign terrorist attack on American soil since Pearl Harbour. The news channels were eager to show the damage but did not go into much detail about the men who did it, preferring to describe them as a "small foreign faction".

And television itself was also trying to deal with a different type of foreign faction. Home computer sales had been growing slowly but steadily for the last years, mostly for small businesses. But then someone realised the microchips could be made far more cheaply and far quicker in far east countries that did not have minimum wages and unions. *Windows 95* made headline news when it went on sale and quickly sold out in many stores across the country, confusing and surprising many people who had no idea what it was. Bill Gates, a university drop out and associate of financier Jeffrey Epstein, created the first home computer system that could easily be linked to the internet. The world wide web had been designed so that academics would be able to speak to each other from all over the world and that philosophical ideas could be shared in a global living room. Unfortunately, its rise was due to more baser instincts most likely to be found in the virtual bedroom. The real thrust behind the growth of home computer sales were violent games and pornography.

The video footage of her lipstick smile and the blonde hair made her a sensation on the internet even though she never wanted it to be this way. People could sit at home and rewatch her time and time again. Pamela Anderson and Tommy Lee Jones had made a "sex tape" for their own private viewing. When it was stolen, the *Baywatch* beauty found that once something goes online it's almost impossible to remove it. News of the story and images of her from the video increased the number of people dialling up to use the internet, making companies such as John Ramsey's Access Graphics a lot of money, and Pamela even more famous. People who would never admit they had seen the footage somehow knew everything about miss Anderson.

But as well as hundreds of adult porn sites available, there was also a darker world for anyone who was willing to look deeper. The internet was a Pandora's Box that once opened there was little anyone could do to stop the horrors of the virtual world from being unleashed. 1995 saw the FBI carry out the first big series of raids across America titled *Operation Innocent*. This was a multitasked crackdown to try and stop the spread of indecent images of young children. The nation was shocked at just how many people were caught. At least the mainstream media such as television would never try to appeal to the public's baser instincts in such a way.

The trial of O.J. Simpson was to be televised from start to finish. Why the prosecution agreed to this was a mistake. The Simpson defence team argued and harassed the prosecution until most of the jury were black. The prosecution, believing that a woman, even if they were black, would see the truth and stand up for justice, was another mistake. Then there was the kicking out of important witnesses. One woman who had seen a white Bronco driven by a black male near to the crime scene was dismissed due to selling her account to a tabloid magazine. The prosecution relinquished again, believing that even the circumstantial evidence would be enough to secure a conviction. The Simpson Defence Team had already decided O.J. was never going to give evidence and be cross examined. This was not going to be a trial about people; it was going to be all about DNA.

Those who had never heard of DNA at the start of the trial would consider themselves experts by the end of it. The prosecution spoke about blood, the defence told the jury about movable objects. The prosecution spoke about evidence, the defence talked about contamination. The prosecution spoke about cells being linked to other cells;

the defence spoke about racism. These were the early years of DNA being part of an investigation, and it would be fair to say mistakes were made by the police at the crime scenes. But they believed DNA found among the body of his dead wife matched that of O.J. Simpson, and they were probably right. For Simpsons expensive defence team, they also knew that the average jury member wouldn't understand much about DNA, and so decided to use ordinary language as a weapon to manipulate the narrative of what happened that night. They would be more right. A man goes to see his wife and children a few days before is bound to leave DNA at the house.

The Simpson Defence Team then focused on detective Mark Fuhrman, the man who had been to both the crime scene and Simpson address that night (without a warrant). Fuhrman was prepared to be asked about police procedure. Instead he was asked about the word "nigger" and if he had ever said it, Fuhrman replied that he had not, unsure of what this had to do with a murder trial. The defence then played recordings from a few years previously in which Fuhrman said that word a couple of times. After that the defence argued that it was impossible to take what he said as the truth. The glove, the blood, even the cut on Simpson's hand, were all tainted because of something Fuhrman had said five years prior. But even with his evidence called into question, many Americans, including Patsy Ramsey, believed that Simpson would be found guilty.

The Simpson Defence Team kept playing mind games. Before the jury visited Simpsons home, all his "white" art was replaced with black and tribal works of art. All photographs of him with his famous white friends were replaced with historical black figures. With Simpson refusing to take the stand and answer any questions, the prosecution was left asking experts for their opinion; to which the Simpson Defence Team would bring out their own experts to say the other expert's opinion was wrong. The prosecution then made another mistake and produced the leather glove that had shrunk and stiffened over time and said that it was O'J's. The defence kept it simple: If the glove doesn't fit, you've got to acquit. O.J. who had stopped taking his arthritic medication, which made his hands swell, pushed out his fingers until they were stiff and pretended he could not get the glove on his hand.

The judge gave no directions. The mostly black jury decided that the black Simpson was innocent of murdering two white people. Some believed that after the riots a few years previously when police officers accused of beating Rodney King were set free no politician was going to complain. Others believed they had seen too many innocent black men sent to prison while guilty white men escaped conviction. White America was stunned but did not riot. They believed he had got away with it because he had the same genetic make-up as most of the jury. I disagree. I think it was because Simpson was rich. His expensive defence team showed that someone could escape from justice within the definition of the law. In legal terms O.J. Simpson was innocent. The two deaths are still unsolved, but the police are not looking for any other suspects. When the verdict was announced Patsy Ramsey came out and said to her gardener, "Now you can get away with murder in this country". The trial would cast its shadow over the JonBenét Ramsey investigation for the next thirty years.

In January 1996, a nine-year-old girl named Amber Hagerman was abducted while riding her bike. She was found dead a few days later with severe neck injuries. Her parents helped the police all they could until the case began to grow cold, and they then decided that more should be done. They were not rich, but they campaigned relentlessly to change the law in relation to child abductions and sex offenders. Eventually they helped introduce "Amber Alerts", where radio stations and freeway signs would be used to identify possible abductors. They also went to Congress to ask for a National Database of registered Sex

Offenders. They have never stopped campaigning for justice. The killer of their daughter has still not been identified.

Chapter 3

December, spelt DNA, DNR.

Things fall apart; the centre cannot hold;

Mere anarchy is loosed upon the world,

The blood-dimmed tide is loosed, and everywhere

The ceremony of innocence is drowned;

The best lack all conviction, while the worst

Are full of passionate intensity.

W. B. Yeats, *The Second Coming.*

December 1996. John Ramsey had worked hard all year and was looking forward to seeing his two other children from a previous marriage, a son, and a daughter, now adults. They were all planning to meet at the Ramsey's holiday home in Chicago on the 26th. But there was a sadness behind this. There had been a third child, another daughter, who had been killed a few years previously in a car crash. It was a total accident, but it had tested John's faith. How does a father cope with losing his child when

God is meant to be watching over them. How do you deal with all the hospital forms, the autopsy report, the funeral arrangements, and the anniversaries that will never be celebrated again?

As a follower of the Episcopal Church, John believed it was the spirit of a person that went to Heaven. The body was just a vessel while here on Earth. With something such as brain death, even if a body was still technically kept alive by machine, the person/personality had already joined the angels. Patsy was also a believer in Heaven. She may have had even more reason to question her faith than John. In 1993 Patsy had been diagnosed with Stage 4 ovarian cancer, often considered terminal. Patsy decided to fight it and went through extensive chemotherapy treatment, spending many days away from her young family. The spare bedroom next to JonBenét's was turned into a treatment room. After a year the cancer went into remission. She was to later say that an Angel had told her she was going to survive. Now both she and John shared a bond of having been close to death, and both had got through it because of their faith.

They had moved to Boulder Colorado after JonBenét was born. It was the sort of place where every other front lawn flew the stars and stripes. Statistically it had a high rate of burglaries and bicycle thefts. This was because of the University of Colorado was also located here. Most burglaries were items being taken from dorm rooms. Students would also leave the bikes around the town, and if it had gone when they came back, they usually took someone else's. The police took a relaxed view when recording these crimes. They knew what was happening, but Boulder was a rich comfortable white town, and in the end the students' parents would usually resolve the issue.

The Ramseys had a party at the start of December to celebrate John's birthday. Afterwards JonBenét went to another pageant competition, then she and Patsy stopped in New York to see some shows and do some shopping. John and *Access Graphics* appeared in the local paper on the 21st of December, after the company was believed to have turned over a billion dollars in revenue that year. Now in his fifties, no doubt he was hoping to spend more time sailing and flying, things he had done when he was at a Naval base in the Philippines years ago.

JonBenét had won a few beauty pageant competitions that year, enough for her to appear in the local mall. This included her singing *Rockin around the Christmas Tree*, wearing a red outfit. She then appeared in the Boulder Christmas parade on the 22nd of December, sitting in a sleigh being driven through the streets as she waved at the crowds. At this point we should take a moment to highlight two factors: First, the investigation into her death is still ongoing. As such, I don't know if any information is being kept out of public knowledge as it may be significant. The other factor is that when it comes to DNA and clothing fibres, transference can last a few days. It's possible the DNA that was to be found under JonBenét's fingernails could have got there from now on.

It could have also got there on the 23rd when the Ramseys had another party. I sometimes wonder if Patsy liked large parties because there were more intimate than smaller ones. The house was certainly big enough to entertain a lot of visitors. The detached property had four floors, including a basement, a ground floor with a kitchen pantry and access to a large garage, two staircases up to the next floor where JonBenét and Burke's had their bedrooms, JonBenét having an ensuite bathroom and a balcony. There were also two staircases to the top floor. This was the master bedroom of John and Patsy. It had walk in wardrobes, a fireplace, and two bathrooms. The house was so big that Patsy liked to have ten Christmas trees in it. The trees were usually kept in the basement in a room called the "wine cellar". There were no bottles. What it did have was an old-fashioned wooden block latch nailed on the top of the door frame. This allowed John and Patsy to store presents in there without the kids finding them. Also in the basement was the children's games room, filled with shelves of toys and a model railway on a large table. There were other rooms in the basement and a laundry area. The house was so big, if you walked around the outside you would have no way of knowing if somebody was in a room on the other side unless you crossed the garden to look.

The party on the 23rd of December included children from the neighbourhood, and a local man playing Santa, Bill McReynolds. Years ago, his daughter was abducted with a friend and the friend was sexually assaulted in a basement. Bill's wife went on the write a play about the adduction, changing the story to have a young girl strangled to death. Now older, Bill had grown a long white beard and long white hair. Some of the kids thought he was the real Santa. But he was hiding another secret. His recent heart surgery restricted a lot of his movement as he played Santa Claus. It was also at this party that an odd thing occurred. At 6.47pm someone rang the operator then hung up. Police returned the call, but only got the answering machine. A police car arrived at the home within six minutes. It was believed John's friend Fleet White had called by mistake.

On Christmas Eve the family went to the Nativity at their local Episcopal church, with lessons by Pastor Rol Hoverstock. They then drove around the town looking at the Christmas lights before having a meal at a local restaurant. A light flurry of snow began to fall. After they got home John went over to a neighbour, the Barnfield's, to collect the bike for JonBenét. I don't know where the bike Patsy got for Christmas had been kept. Burke already had a bike that was kept in the garage (perhaps John had one there too). There were a couple of old creeks that ran down to Chautauqua Park five minutes' walk away. Once you had crossed Columbine Avenue there were several cycle routes you could use.

On Christmas morning Burke got up first. It was still early. He then woke JonBenét. They went up the stairs to their parents' bedroom to wake them. Then they all went downstairs to open the presents. There are pictures of Burke, JonBenét and Patsy by the Christmas tree, including one of JonBenét with her bike and one with Patsy (in pyjamas with no make-up) looking happy with her daughter. After a breakfast of pancakes some of the neighbourhood kids arrived. John went to the local airport to arrange their flight for the next day and load the plane. When he came back, he watched JonBenét ride her bike (Burke was not to get a new one until a few weeks later).

They got ready for the party at Fleet White's house. Patsy would comment that JonBenét had a bit of a tantrum because she refused to wear the same clothes as her mother, red turtleneck top and black trousers. Instead, JonBenét wore a white top and black waistcoat with black pants. The family got there around 5pm. They ate a seafood buffet and played games with other children. They leave later that night (the times vary), stopping of at their friends, the Stine's, and the Walkers, to drop off Christmas gifts, with Patsy speaking to Glen and Susan Stine for about ten minutes.

From here we will use the first accounts that were given to the police by John and Patsy. From Officer Rick French, who wrote his report on the 26th of December, he stated that the Ramseys told him they arrived home at 10pm. John read to both children and they were in bed by 10.30pm (it does not say if he read to them in their own bedrooms). Patsy tells officer French that JonBenét had been put to bed dressed in long white underwear and a red turtleneck top.

From detective Linda Arndt's report, written on 8th January, "John had read to JonBenét after she had gone to bed". This information could have been given to Arndt by officer French, so there may have been some miscommunication. But later Arndt does speak to John in person, and he tells her that they got home approx. 10pm, that Patsy and Burke immediately went to bed, and that he had read to JonBenét and tucked her into bed at approx. 10.30pm. John then went to bed and took a sleeping pill.

Its Christmas night. Some families are still up, but there are no bars or restaurants open. The streets are quiet. We now have the possibility that someone is near the house planning to kidnap a child. We know that JonBenét died sometime between 11pm and 1am. The clock is ticking. The kidnapper waits. They wait until they believe the world is asleep. A rough beast slouches towards the basement window.

That night JonBenét received a series of injuries. There are the marks on the side of the face and back, her skull is fractured, there are marks around her vagina which are difficult to give an innocent account for, there is cord tied around her hands, another cord had been tied around her neck. Even today we still don't know in what order they occurred. One neighbour reported that they heard the sound of something metallic being dropped onto the concrete. A different neighbour believed they looked out around midnight and saw the kitchen light on, which was strange as the Ramseys had never done that before. Another neighbour believed they heard a scream between 1 and 2am. They even went so far as to say that it was the loud scream of a child. It occurred only once, and then there was silence. At some point it also stopped snowing.

Chapter 4

Footnotes on the Stairs.

We all want to forget something, so we tell stories. It's easier that way.

Rashomon. Directed by Akira Kurosawa 1950

At around 5.40am on the 26th of December Patsy told police that she walked down in the darkness and saw it, or rather them. Three pieces of note paper had been placed evenly across one whole step. Patsy walked over them, turned around and looked at the first few lines.

[ATTACHMENT A]

Mr. Ramsey,

Listen carefully! We are a group of individuals that represent a small foreign faction. We do respect your bussiness but not the country that it serves. At this time we have your daughter in our posession. She is safe and unharmed and if you want her to see 1997, you must follow our instructions to the letter.

You will withdraw $118,000.00 from your account. $100,000 will be in $100 bills and the remaining $18,000 in $20 bills. Make sure that you bring an adequate size attache to the bank. When you get home you will put the money in a brown paper bag. I will call you between 8 and 10 am tomorrow to instruct you on delivery. The delivery will be exhausting so I advise you to be rested. If we monitor you getting the money early, we might call you early to arrange an earlier delivery of the ___

money and hence a earlier
~~delivery~~ pick-up of your daughter.
Any deviation of my instructions
will result in the immediate
execution of your daughter. You
will also be denied her remains
for proper burial. The two
gentlemen watching over your daughter
do not particularly like you so I
advise you not to provoke them.
Speaking to anyone about your
situation, such as Police, F.B.I., etc.,
will result in your daughter being
beheaded. If we catch you talking
to a stray dog, she dies. If you
alert bank authorities, she dies.
If the money is in any way
marked or tampered with, she
dies. You will be scanned for
electronic devices and if any are
found, she dies. You can try to
deceive us but be warned that
we are familiar with law enforcement
countermeasures and tactics. You
stand a 99% chance of killing
your daughter if you try to out
smart us. Follow our instructions

and you stand a 100% chance
of getting her back. You and
your family are under constant
scrutiny as well as the authorities.
Don't try to grow a brain
John. You are not the only
fat cat around so don't think
that killing will be difficult.
Don't underestimate us John.
Use that good southern common
sense of yours. It is up to
you now John!

Victory!

S.B.T.C

I have typed out the message and added numbers to the lines to help clarify certain points.

1.   Mr. Ramsey,

2.   Listen carefully! We are a group of individuals that represent

3.   a small foreign faction. We xx respect your bussiness

4.   but not the country that it serves. At this time we have

5.   your daughter in our possession. She is safe and unharmed and

6.   if you want her to see 1997, you must follow our instructions to

7.   the letter.

8.   You will withdraw $118,000.00 from your account. $100,000 will be

9.   in $100 bills and the remaining $18,000 in $20 bills. Make sure

10.   that you bring an adequate size attaché to the bank. When you get

11.   home you will put the money in a brown paper bag. I will call you

12.   between 8 and 10 am tomorrow to instruct you on delivery. The

13.   delivery will be exhausting so I advise you to be rested. If we

14.   monitor you getting the money early, we might call you early to

15.   arrange an earlier delivery of the money and hence a earlier

16.   ~~delivery~~ pickup of your daughter.

17.   Any deviation of my instructions will result in the immediate

18.   execution of your daughter. You will also be denied her remains

19.   for proper burial. The two gentlemen watching over your daughter

20.   do not particularly like you so I advise you not to provoke them.

21.   Speaking to anyone about your situation, such as Police, F.B.I.,

22.   etc., will result in your daughter being beheaded. If we catch you

23.   talking to a stray dog, she dies. If you alert bank authorities, she

24.   dies. If the money is in any way marked or tampered with, she dies.

25.   You will be scanned for electronic devices and if any are found, she

26.   dies. You can try to deceive us but be warned that we are familiar

27.   with Law enforcement countermeasures and tactics. You stand a 99%

28.   chance of killing your daughter if you try to out smart us. Follow

29.   our instructions and you stand a 100% chance of getting her back.

30.   You and your family are under constant scrutiny as well as the

31.   authorities. Don't try to grow a brain John. You are not the only

32.   fat cat around so don't think that killing will be difficult. Don't

33.   underestimate us John. Use that good southern common sense of yours.

34.   It is up to you now John!

35.   Victory!

36.   S.B.T.C

These three pages constitute the only real evidence we have of the person involved in JonBenét's death. The police would later find out the ransom note had been written in the house, on Patsy's notepad, which was put back on the desk drawer along with the felt tip pen, which was also put back where it was usually kept.

The first line relates only to Mr Ramsey, avoiding Patsy. It then goes on to explain the kidnappers are a "small foreign faction". Would anyone who wanted to strike fear into a victim describe themselves as a "small foreign faction"? And if you are going to describe yourself as belonging to a faction or group, then why not give yourself a name, such as SBTC. The answer could be that the writer is lying, but here is the thing: the clock is ticking. To write out a lie takes more time than simply not including it. So, this type of lie needs to do two things; to make you believe that a small foreign faction wrote it, and to draw you away from anyone you might suspect of writing it. As for lines 4 and 5, if you don't respect a country, why would you respect any business in it unless it. I think this is a reference to Johns company and it links to Lockheed Martin, one of the biggest military companies in the world.

The spelling mistakes in lines 2 and 3 are often cited as being a deliberate attempt by someone trying to hide their intelligence. I think they are just spelling mistakes because the writer is nervous. The writer also never uses the name of JonBenét. John had an elder daughter. You would think they would have made the initial point of letting him know who they had kidnapped. It is also interesting that the writer is trying to hide their personal characteristics by trying not to join the letters together. But rather than write each letter in capitals, they use what is essentially a form of shorthand as if setting out an article for a newspaper, including indents to denote a new paragraph. Line 5 has the word "unharmed", although the writer leaves a space between *un* and *harmed*. Could it be that they already know what's happened to JonBenét?

The writer certainly seems to know a lot about John. The $188,000.00 is the amount he got as a Christmas bonus. I should point out that he got the money in February 1996, so he may not have had that amount in his bank account. The writer also felt the need to describe the amount correctly using a comma and a decimal point. Was this someone familiar with writing large cheques?

Line 10 has the word "*attaché*". I don't think I have ever used the word "*attaché*" in my life. If I did, I would probably have used the phrase "*attaché case*", as it sounds more correct. It turns out the writer was right. Attaché is another word for case, and it is even spelled correctly with an accent above the *e*. But why does the writer need to be so specific? The next point is a question – what time his bank open in 1996? John may have been able to obtain that amount of money quite easily, but he would only be able to do it when the bank was open. And would he be able to get back home between 8 and 10am when they were due to call? All these instructions just seem to be extra work for the police to take them away from the house.

From line 17 we have the threat that any deviation from these instructions will result in his daughter's death. But just a few lines earlier the writer is happy for John to get the money whenever he can. The idea of watching over someone rather than just watching implies that JonBenét is lying down. And why *"gentlemen"*? Men would have carried more of a threat. As for all the threats themselves, I find it strange the writer uses exclamation marks to emphasize certain points for dramatic effect but does not feel the need to add any when threatening to kill John's daughter.

On line 15 the writer uses the phrase *"and hence"*. This is probably a verbal slip and something the writer might say in everyday speech. It's a piece of the jigsaw that gives us a glimpse of who this person might be. On the next line the writer crosses out the word *"delivery"*. Were they expecting JonBenét to be delivered into the hands of the authorities because they knew she was already dead?

From line 17 we have more threats that John's daughter will die. These are excessive and other example of the writer trying to tell us over and over they have JonBenét when time is of the essence. Why? One reason might be because they are not concerned about getting caught (don't forget, this is meant to be an intruder who could be found out at any moment). In line 20 they even make the mistake and must insert the word "not" when saying about John they "*do ... particularly like you*".

The writer becomes more personal at the end, using "*John*" instead of "*Mr Ramsey*". It feels as though they are trying to rule out Patsy from being involved, but they still fail to mention the name of the girl they have kidnapped. On line 22 there is another piece of grammatical complexity that highlights our writer's intellectual capabilities. They use "*etc*", and the correct period of "*.,*". When continuing with a sentence after using the phrase *Et Cetera*, you use the full stop to indicate that your list is essentially ending, and also a comma to indicate the sentence itself is continuing. Most people would have probably ended the sentence on *etc*, but here is someone who has a far greater understanding of English grammar than most of the American population.

The sign off, "S.B.T.C*"* at first glance could mean anything. If it's the name of the foreign faction, why did they not use it at the start of the note? And why does the writer, so grammatically precise throughout, miss the last full stop? Were they expecting something more, did they run out of time, do the initials mean anything? If the writer had moved each letter one to the left, they would have got *R.A.S.B*. Move one letter to the right its *T.C.U.D.* neither has any link to John Ramsey. But John had done his Navy training in the far east, specifically at the Subic Bay Training Centre in the Philippines. He used to have a framed poster of a ship in a harbour which underneath were written the words *Subic Bay Training Centre (SBTC)*. Another interesting factor is that in 1967 when John was doing his Navy training, the Philippine currency still had the word *"Victory"* written on some of the bank notes. The writer must have either had knowledge about John's early life and detailed information about his business life, or they were just extremely lucky.

Since they were first discovered on the spiral staircase, the three pages have continued to divide those who believe it was an intruder, and those who believe someone in the house wrote it. The only sets of fingerprints found on it belonged to a member of the police, and Patsy. John produced handwriting samples and was ruled out of being the writer. Patsy, who was ambidextrous, was asked a few times to produce samples due to its similarity to her writing found on notes and letters inside the home. But there were issues around the examples she submitted. On one occasion Patsy would only submit to a sample if she could do it in the District Attorney's own home, and he went for a walk while John was the only witness to his wife writing a sample. They had also been given a copy of the ransom note. Eventually John and Patsy hired their own handwriting experts, but even they could not rule her out.

Handwriting analysis is not an exact science and so it's open to scrutiny in a court of law. It is also not just about writing style. People look for grammar, the way certain words are linked, the rhythm and cadence of each sentence, and even how certain phrases are put into context. So, perhaps we should be asking if an expert can first tell the difference between male and female writing. It would also be interesting if they believed the ransom note was being dictated by a male and written by a female. Also, can an expert tell if it was written using the right or left-hand, or if someone was wearing gloves? The difficulty with this appears to be the felt tip pen, which distorts the finer points of someone's handwriting. Perhaps the main problem is that someone has tried to disguise their writing. The person who wrote the note would go out of their way to continue to disguise their writing by trying to be as different from the ransom note as possible. The same issue would be with trying to compare the writing in the note to any previous writing. The only thing most of the experts agreed on was that although the start of the ransom note is someone trying to hide their style, the last few paragraphs would more likely be their normal style. But it raises the question: If it was an intruder, why would they try and disguise their writing in the first place. Wouldn't it have been far easier to make the note as short as possible if they thought the Ramsey's might recognise it?

But there is something in the ransom note which helps narrow down the list of suspects. By its content it's clear that this is a person of at least a high school education and must have included studying a literature-based subject. We could go even further and say this was someone who had been to university.

Starting with the possibility there are a thousand suspects, let's say that forty percent of them do not have a university education. We can lose four hundred people. Ten percent gained a degree outside of a literature-based subject, so lose another hundred people. That's half our suspects gone (don't forget, both intruder theorists and Ramsey theorists believe that the killer wrote the ransom note). Sex, we don't know, but if we say the writer was between the age of twenty to sixty, we can rule out another fifty people. If we say that Christmas night would exclude another fifty from our list due to them having family commitments or being too far away to be able to commit the crime, we go down to 400 suspects. How many of those left knew he had a daughter, had been enough times to get an idea of the layout of the house, knew the neighbourhood well enough to know they would not be seen. More importantly, how many people within John's business and social circle would be psychologically capable of committing a crime? I would suggest we can discount a further three hundred people. Now it's only a hundred suspects. How many knew the family were going away on the 26th and so the only night to commit the crime was Christmas night; lose twenty. How many knew John got a Christmas bonus of 118k that year, lose another twenty. How many knew the alarm system would not be on, and more importantly, knew it did not cover the basement, lose another thirty. How many were confident enough to be in the house for possibly up to an hour, be able to walk around in the dark, and knew if John had a gun or not, lose twenty-eight. We are now down to only two suspects who had the means, motivation, and opportunity to write this note.

It also feels that parts of the ransom note are being dictated rather than the writer expressing their own thoughts. This leads us to the possibility of two people being involved in writing the note. Or let's say that the person writing the note was of an above average intelligence and the second person was the more dominant partner. It could also be the reason why the ransom note is so long when the motive is so short. At face value it is a kidnapper demanding ransom money. There is the strange notion of only asking for a small amount of $118,00.00 (precise enough for a comma and decimal point). This implies the writer had knowledge of Johns Christmas bonus, which could be seen as a clue for police to start looking at Johns business life. But even if you were an estranged former employee of Access Graphics, wouldn't you be demanding more? If John had been in the papers recently because his company turned over a billion dollars that year, why not ask for a million? It may have been because the kidnapper was hoping not to get the police involved; but it also seems that the amount is there for the readers benefit than the kidnappers. And surely if this was written by someone involved with Johns company, the last thing they would do would be to demand a ransom amount that the police would quickly link to anyone employed by John.

When I look at the wording and its links to various films such as *Dirty Harry* and *Speed*, I don't think a movie fan wrote it. Even though it was 1996, I think someone was using the internet to look for those quotes. I also think they put in "kidnap threats" rather than "ransom notes" into the search engine. John had a computer in his study. This would be the years when you had to dial into the internet rather than use wi-fi.

There is also another question: was the ransom note written before or after JonBenét had died (or even mortally injured)? Would a kidnapper break into a home and write the note before they had taken JonBenét from her bed, then kill her before they had left the house? Otherwise, why write a ransom note. The same would be true if it was written after JonBenét had died. Why spend what is believed to be over twenty minutes writing out a note that is of no financial benefit to you whatsoever, and of caught you would be arrested for murder and face the death penalty? At this point we should also mention the police were to later find the start of another ransom note (called The Practice Note) in the house, raising the possibility the writer had made a few attempts to get the wording right. So, whether JonBenét was alive or dead, someone needed to write that note, but they didn't take the practice note with them. It may be because they didn't care, but I think it's because the ransom note had to be finished before 6am. If we say death occurred between 10.30pm and 1am it means a person could have waited six hours to calm down, and then taken over an hour to write those three pages, deliberately trying to disguise their own handwriting. And it would have helped if someone else was dictating parts of the ransom note to them rather than having to think about what they were writing. Perhaps the ultimate clue as to the identity of the writer is is at the very start of the ransom note – *Listen carefully*.

Chapter 5

The Phone Call.

She... (we gave her most of our lives)

Is leaving... (sacrificed most of our lives)

Home... (we gave her everything money could buy)

    The Beatles, *She's leaving Home.*

From the longest ransom note in history we come to one of
the shortest telephone calls regarding a mother and a
missing child. We have a sequence of events: Patsy has got
up at approx. 5.30am (but not had a shower), got fully
dressed (not known if she was wearing the same shoes as
the night before), put on make-up, and has come down the
first set of stairs past JonBenét's bedroom and washed one
of JonBenét's clothes in the sink by the laundry area. She
has then gone down the spiral staircase (in the dark?), has
stepped over the three pages placed neatly on a lower step,
and has turned and looked at part of the ransom note (still
in the dark?). After reading the first few lines she has then

jumped back over the pages, has gone up the stairs and looked in JonBenét's bedroom, realised that JonBenét was not in her bed, and has then called for John. You would think that the normal reaction would be to call her daughter's name or even check the room. Instead, Patsy has run across the length of the house and looked in Burke's bedroom (in the dark) but has not asked him any questions or called out for JonBenét. If Patsy had called for her husband earlier, it's surprising that Burke did not as any questions at least come out to see what was going on.

Patsy has then gone back along to the other side of the house and back down the spiral staircase, again stepping over the ransom note. We must then assume she does not read the note as she waits for John to come down from the bedroom. He appears just in a pair of boxer shorts, places the ransom note on the floor and tells Patsy to call the police. She gets put through to the operator at 5.52am. There is some controversy over whether she first tries to ask for an ambulance and then changes her mind. Here is the transcript of that call.

Patsy: (mumbles something which sounds like the beginning of ambulance and then stops) Police?

911: What's going on ma'am?

Patsy: 755 15th street.

911: What's going on there, ma'am?

Patsy: We have a kidnapping. Hurry, please!

911: Explain to me what's going on. Ok?

Patsy: There. We have a, there's a note left, and our daughter's gone.

911: A note was left, and your daughter's gone?

Patsy: Yes!

911: How old is your daughter?

Patsy: She's 6 years old. She's blonde, 6 years old.

911: How long ago was this?

Patsy: I don't know. I just got the note, and my daughter's gone.

911: Does it say who took her?

Patsy: What?

911: Does it say who took her?

Patsy: No! I don't know. There's a, there's a ransom note here.

911: It's a ransom note?

Patsy: It says SBTC. Victory! Please!

911: Okay, what's your name? Are you Kath...?

Patsy: Patsy Ramsey, I'm the mother. Oh my God! Please!

911: Okay, I'm sending an officer over, OK?

Patsy: Please!

911: Do you know how long she's been gone?

Patsy: No I don't! Please, we just got up and she's not here. Oh my god! Please!

911: Okay, Cal....

Patsy: Please send somebody.

911: I am honey.

Patsy: Please.

911: Take a deep breath and...

Patsy: Hurry, hurry, hurry!

911: Patsy? Patsy? Patsy? Patsy…?

But Patsy has already ended the call.

There are now three significant points where JonBenét's name is never mentioned. The first is in the ransom note, the second is when Patsy realises JonBenét is not in her bed but only calls out for John, and the last is the phone call itself. It's almost as if both the writer of the ransom note and Patsy cannot bear to say her name. Some people believe that any mother will immediately tell the operator their missing child's name in the hope that the police may already have them; so Patsy's avoidance to give the operator the most basic description of her daughter, her name, is strange. Patsy points out that "we have a kidnapping" and that "our daughters gone", again distancing herself from the name of JonBenét, and it also depersonalises Patsy herself. It's not *My child had been kidnapped,* or *My daughters gone.* Nor does Patsy give any details of when JonBenét was last seen or what she was wearing, only that there is a note and again that her daughter has gone. The repetition of the word "gone", as opposed to "missing", could also imply that the house has already been searched, or something slightly more sinister.

If Patsy is standing by the spiral staircase using the wall telephone, she must either be able to still see the note or is close enough to John for him to say to her what's on the note, as she tells the operator the people who took her have ended the message with *SBTC* and *Victory.* Patsy was to state later that on that day, she never read the ransom note in full, so it's strange how and why she got the last two lines in the wrong order. The answer may be that John is able to hear the conversation and is giving Patsy information as she speaks.

Patsy is the first to hang up rather than wait for the operator to finish asking questions. Most parents whose children have gone missing will stay with the operator for as long as possible to try and get all the help they can. It feels as though Patsy terminates the call so that she doesn't have to answer any more questions. Although we should give Patsy a certain amount of leeway as we cannot say what we would do if we were in her shoes. This is why the intruder theory still holds weight in relation to the phone call, although there is something else that happens which makes me question that narrative.

It was not until twenty years later that the controller was finally spoken to. As someone who did have years of experience, she made the telling point that something wasn't quite right with the call. Not with what Patsy had said, but her behaviour between the lines. The panic in her voice seemed to come and go whenever Patsy felt that it was needed. So much so, the controller did something they don't usually do, and kept their end of the line open. And here we come to the next part of the mystery.

After Patsy has hung up, the controller believes she hears Patsy say, "Okay, we've called the police, now what?" It then sounded like there were two voices in the background, perhaps three. Over the years there have been many attempts to try and find out what is said. One theory is that Patsy can be heard saying "Help me Jesus," which would be understandable. And if there is another voice that can be heard, we must remember John is reading the ransom note nearby. Any concerned father would immediately be asking what was happening to find his daughter. And if Patsy does turn around and ask John what to do next, this could also be seen as a normal reaction.

The issue seems to be with the possibility of a third voice. This could only be Burke. Some people believe that he asks his parents "What did you find?" Or, he says something and Patsy replies, "Baby, what did you do, what did you do?" If it was Burke, it would seem natural that after he heard his mother call out for his father he would come out and see what was happening. After all, he was expecting to get up early to fly to Michigan. He could have stood on the spiral staircase to hear his mother speaking into the phone and his father crouched down on the floor reading something. For him to ask, "What did you find?" seems like a reasonable question. Even the reply "We're not talking to you" could be a normal reaction from a father dealing with a traumatic situation. The problem is both Patsy and John told police that day that Burke had been asleep in bed all morning. When Burke was interviewed a few weeks later he also claimed to have stayed in his bedroom until he went to Fleet White's house at around 7am.

For me this is another part of the narrative that doesn't fit the evidence. Or to be more precise, its where the Ramseys are giving stories that do not make sense. If Burke had come down and asked a question, would it have made any difference to the investigation? At the the Ramseys had no way of knowing that the controller had kept the line open. As soon as officer French arrived John and Patsy told him that Burke was asleep upstairs. Within

the hour Burke is taken straight out of his bedroom and to
Fleet White's house before any detective gets the chance to
speak to him. it was not later that the call was examined,
long after the Ramseys had stuck to their story of Burke
staying in his bedroom that morning. If they changed it
now, they would look extremely suspicious. But if they
were lying at the time, the only gain would be to somehow
save themselves, or Burke.

In truth, the experts cannot give a definitive answer as
to what was said. We cannot even conclusively prove that
there are three voices in the background. The recording
was taken from an analogue tape system in the control
room. This non-digital format would have included
background sounds in the control room and white noise on
the tape itself. So, the best evidence we have is the
controller herself. She is directly linked to the phone
receiver at the Ramseys house via a set of headphones. If
she thinks she hears three voices, she probably did. And
perhaps we should go back to the controller's initial
concerns; about not so much Patsy was saying, but the
silence as she waited for the controller to speak. Patsy tells
the controller to *hurry, hurry, hurry*, and then when she
believes she has hung up…she goes back to being silent.
But there should be voices once the call has ended. Patsy is
standing by John who is on the floor reading the last of the

ransom note, both should have been asking questions straight away. It's the foreboding silence in the thirty seconds of dead air that is more suspicious than any possible voices heard in the background.

When finally interviewed in 2016, the controller said soon after investigators (for the Ramseys?) told her she could be summoned to give evidence in any future trial and was threatened with arrest if she ever spoke publicly about the call. She went on to say that as an experienced controller she wanted to keep Patsy on the line and try to get as much information as possible to help the police. At some point she would have asked for the daughter's name. That should not be an issue. But what if the controller, someone dealing with a report of a missing child, who doesn't know the full details of the ransom note, who doesn't know who the father is, who doesn't know how big Patsy's home is, then asks another straightforward question, "Have you searched every room in the house"? It was unfortunate that the controller was unable to keep listening, as Patsy then started to make other calls rather than look for her daughter.

Chapter 6

If Six was One.

I hate to break it to you but there is no big lie, there is no system. The universe is indifferent.

Don Draper, Mad Men.

Perhaps the reason the police never fully searched the house was because they assumed the parents had already done it. Officer Rick French reports that when he arrived five minutes after Patsy had called, John and patsy were both fully dressed. John told him there were no obvious signs of forced entry. The alarm had not been turned on, but the house looked the same as when he locked up the night before. It's quite possible police assumed the place had already been searched. The Ramsey's told officer French it was a kidnap and there was a ransom note. It appeared to everyone that the little girl had gone. But this does not exclude the police from being unaccountable. They should have carried out a full search. One reason this appears not to have been done was because they were told that the Ramseys were an influential family and to treat them with deference. If they said their child had been kidnapped, it was a kidnap. Another reason was an order for strict radio silence in case the kidnappers were listening into the police frequency. Finally, with people within the Boulder police force being away for Christmas, the chain of command was broken, and those at the house did not know who was in control. This means there were large periods when the clock was ticking but nothing seemed to be happening.

The phone call to the police is at 5.52am. Patsy then phones her friends the White's and the Fernie's to tell them what has happened and asks them to come over. The police are not aware of these calls when they arrive at around 5.58am. It is still dark. Officer French is given a quick account and checks the ground floor for any signs of a break in. He also makes a brief look around the basement but does not go into the wine cellar as the wooden latch along the top of the door is still in place, which means no one escaped through that room. I'm not sure if he looks in the games room as his report makes no mention of the broken window or the suitcase. It is also not clear if John goes into the basement with the officer. There is another officer outside. They notice there are no footprints in the snow leading to and from the house. Another officer takes the ransom note back to the police station. Barbara and John Fernie arrive. Officer French is unable to make his superiors aware as no officer has a mobile phone. Forensic officers arrive. Fleet and Priscilla White then arrive. The only thing officer French can tell the Ramseys is that the FBI have been informed and detectives will be here once they have collected the phone trap equipment for when the kidnappers ring. No one goes into JonBenét's bedroom apart from the forensic team. At this point only officer French has been down to the basement. But then things then start to gain a momentum of their own.

Fleet White stated he went down the basement and into the games room sometime before 7am. I don't know if it was because John had mentioned anything about not searching the house. Fleet sees the suitcase and a piece of glass on the carpet, which he puts on the windowsill. Fleet is not overly suspicious about the window because he believes it is too small for anyone to climb through and there is a cast iron weather grate outside which he doesn't know if its locked or not. Patsy would later say in an interview that it was her rather than the housemaid who had cleaned up the broken glass a few months prior to Christmas. How did she miss a palm sized piece of glass clearly seen in the police photographs unless it had fallen out that night?

Fleet then goes past the boiler room, which had a small window, and to the wine cellar. He turns the piece of wood acting as a latch and looks in but does not see the body (I don't know if he has ever given a statement in which he sees the white blanket). Quite possibly there is no natural light and as Fleet does not know where the light switches are he is just hoping to find a child more by luck than design. He closes the door and turns the latch back. He goes up and mentions to John Fernie about the broken window, but not the police.

John and Patsy say that they were due to go to the airport for around 6.30 - 7am. How were they planning to get there? Was it by their own car, a taxi, or was the pilot going to pick them up. They had a jeep and a Jaguar in the garage. In fact, they had a vehicle collection worth more than what the kidnappers were demanding for JonBenét. But there are people on the move.

Burke finally gets up, although he does not see anyone. He is dressed and taken straight out of the house around 7am with John Fernie and Fleet White to go to the White's home. Why the Ramseys felt that after their daughter had been kidnapped by a foreign faction that their son would be safe out of their sight I don't know. This was not a decision made by the police, who would have undoubtedly wanted to have asked him a few questions about last night. But again, no one seems to be in charge. Around the same time the Ramsey's Pastor, Rol Hoverstock, arrived after being called by someone that morning. Now we have people coming, people going, people coming back, and the police unable to tell their bosses what's happening because of strict radio silence.

John Fernie and Fleet White return around 7.45am. What John had been doing during this time we don't know. He was to later state that at some point in the morning he also searched the basement, although not the wine cellar. He sees the suitcase, and he believes the broken window was open, so he closes it to stop any draught, but does not tell anyone. There are a few things odd about this. The first is that I am not sure what John is looking for as he must have known officer French and Fleet White had already searched the basement. The next is why John felt the need to close a window that already has a big hole in it, as it is hardly going to keep out the cold. There is no inner windowsill. So, John must have moved the piece of glass put there by Fleet. The fourth and most bizarre thing is that John then went upstairs and decided not to tell the police about what he had seen and done. During this time, you had forensic officers looking for clues and no one had yet discovered how the kidnapper got in or out. The biggest issue with all this is that when interviewed later John could not recall the exact time he went into the basement. We must presume he didn't do it between eight and ten when detective Arndt was with him while they waited for the phone call. He could have done it just before 8am when Fleet and John Fernie had left with Burke. He could also have done it around 11am after a lot of officers had left and he disappeared for ninety minutes. Either way, if he thought the open window was odd at the time, he should have told someone at the time.

Detective Arndt arrived at 8.10am along with other detectives. John Fernie knew the local bank manager and so left to arrange the collection of the money. Patsy will spend all morning waiting in the Sunroom while John went anywhere but there. Arndt was to comment that John seemed very distant from Patsy and didn't seem to make any attempt to comfort her. This may be because he is now waiting for the phone call. The phone in John's office is linked to a machine that will trace where the call is coming from. John has given Arndt his mobile phone to use so she can call the police station. The clock is ticking. Everyone waits.

Arndt then made another observation she felt was significant put in her police report. 10am comes and goes and neither John nor Patsy asks her what's happening. The kidnappers' instructions were crystal clear: if the Ramsey's did not strictly comply with the kidnappers demands, their child would be killed. John and Patsy had already broken the first rule by calling the police. Why John, who seemed to have decided to call the police before he had finished reading all the ransom note did not call them on his mobile phone and demand plain clothes detectives or the FBI is a mystery. John also had no issues with someone else going to the bank to collect the money; so again, this is another instruction that had not been carried out. Surely most parents would be asking what happens now?

Maybe other things that morning were of a greater significance. At some point a detective asked for examples of John and Patsy's handwriting as a matter of routine by the FBI. John went to the desk by the spiral staircase and gave the detective two paper pads; one used by John, the other used by Patsy. The pads contained messages from phone calls. John may not have understood it at the time, but rather than rip out a page, the detective took both notepads back to the police station because it was the FBI which had requested them. It was to transpire that Patsy's notepad was used to write the ransom note.

Around 10.30 the forensic team had finished in JonBenét's bedroom and the spiral staircase. They still had not found the point of entry/exit. John kept quiet, so no one had yet linked the broken window in the basement with the kidnapping. John and Patsy had both voiced their concerns over the housekeeper, Linda Hoffman, as she had a key; and one or two former employees of Access graphics. This had been relayed back to headquarters, and resources were now being diverted to look at these people as potential suspects. Detectives, still believing this was a kidnapping, began to leave. The FBI were waiting at the station to hold a briefing. Radio silence had so far made it impossible to get the big picture of what had happened and what was known so far. Every kidnapping is a possible a cross border offence, and so the FBI were technically in charge of the investigation, for the time being.

By 10.45am Det. Linda Arndt was the only officer at the address. There are seven other people left in the house: John, Patsy, the Fernies, the White's, and Pastor Hoverstock. At this point Arndt would not see John for another ninety minutes. She is adamant that for a certain amount of time he is not in the house. I don't know if the garbage was collected on that day, or there are storm drains nearby, an outhouse in the garden, or maybe he could have finally checked the garage. John was to later state that at some point he went to get the post, then read the mail in his office. But this does not account for the other ninety minutes.

Arndt was so concerned that she used the mobile phone to call the police station around 12.30 to say she had not seen John for well over an hour. Due to the policy of no radio traffic, she had to go through a controller first and then find someone in the office to pick up the phone; but everyone was in a meeting. It took a while until the message was relayed back to the FBI. When John finally appears, Arndt contacts the station again (it would be interesting to know if John was aware she was on the phone to the FBI, and that they were planning on getting to the address in the next thirty minutes). The FBI tell Linda Arndt to keep an eye on John and keep him busy until they arrive. Perhaps the plan was for them to speak to him about things he may not wish to admit in front of his wife, such as: are you having an affair, do you owe money, do you have a drug or gambling problem? All of these would have been asked to help narrow down the kidnapper, and the same would have also been asked of Patsy when they spoke to her alone.

Arndt requested more help. John was behaving erratically, the people in the address were becoming very anxious, there was talk of more people coming over (John's son and daughter from his first marriage were on their way to the address, along with the daughter's boyfriend). There have been phone calls from other people that no one has yet checked, and outside there are neighbours wondering what is happening. Arndt must have been feeling as though she has been left on a train of anxious passengers stuck in a snowdrift. The only strange thing was that John and Patsy were not asking any questions about what was happening in relation to their daughter. Arndt followed the FBI's instructions and in front of Fleet White, John was asked to check the house from top to bottom, excluding JonBenét's bedroom, for anything belonging to JonBenét that had been taken or left behind. This was meant to be with Detective Arndt. Before Arndt could ask him to wait while she took another phone call, John took Fleet by the arm and headed straight towards the basement. The investigation had been ongoing for just over seven hours. It was almost 1pm. The kidnapper has never called back.

We are now with John and Fleet as they go down the steps and into the basement. Next to them is a small bathroom. To their left is the boiler room and then the wine cellar. They go straight on and first check the storage space past the laundry area. This has a sink and a washing machine. There are no windows along this part of the house. The floor is filled with junk and old furniture. It's pretty clear the children do not play in this room. There is a large cupboard, but this is not opened. They then go back, past another large cupboard which is not opened. They go into the games room. It is here that John tells Fleet about the strange positioning of the suitcase under the window. I don't know if Fleet tells him he had also been in the basement that morning, and that he had also opened the wine cellar door and seen nothing. The games room has an old lift shaft and engine block which have been turned into cupboards. These are not opened.

They walk past a model train set laid out on the table (with some pieces of track lying on the floor), go out and turn right towards the boiler room. Here is a large freezer and an old furnace. The is a thin window, too small for anyone to climb through. At the end of this room is the wine cellar. John twists the latch off the wine cellar door. Why John decided to look into this room when it has no exit and JonBenét could not have reached the latch, I don't know. But he has been asked by police to check the house before the FBI arrive and that's exactly what he is doing. He opens the wine cellar door. Fleet believes John cried out even before he turned the light on, but we are talking seconds.

We don't know if the body was positioned to send some sort of message from the killer. We don't know how close she was to the door, or if footprints were around the body. We don't know how much of the body was covered by the large white blanket she was wrapped in. We know that she was lying flat on her back, head tilted slightly to the side, and her arms were stretched out above her head. But we don't know why Fleet had not seen the same thing when he had looked in the wine cellar just a few hours before. John has bent over and pulled away the duct tape that covered her mouth to see if she was alive. Although he was criticised for this, I don't blame him.

John then carried the body out of the wine cellar. Perhaps the strangest thing about this was the way he did it. Arndt reported that she saw John carry the child, holding her upright by the waist with his arms outstretched. JonBenet was in full rigor mortis and it was clear she had been dead for a while. Arndt asked John to put the body down, which he did, on the rug in the hallway. After Arndt confirmed JonBenét was dead, John then picked the body up, carried in into the living room, and put it on the floor near the Christmas tree. Before Arndt could do anything, John then placed a throw from an armchair over his daughter and covered her legs with a woollen jumper. Arndt placed the rug up to JonBenét's chin to stop anyone seeing the white cord wrapped around the child's neck. A kidnapping that had looked slightly fictional had become a real murder.

Detective Arndt wrote a full report on 8th January 1997. When she arrived at 8.10am forensic officers were already there, with one of them photographing the outside of the house and another examining JonBenét's bedroom, the one place they knew the kidnapper would have been in. Another forensic officer was checking all possible points of entry on the ground floor for pry marks and fingerprints. Officer French told Arndt that Patsy got up that morning and went down the spiral staircase when she saw the note. She originally thought the note was from the housekeeper (it was 5.30am and that Patsy had used the spiral staircase the night before). The housekeeper had a key for the home and knew they were flying to Michigan that morning. Patsy went on to say the housekeeper had asked for money just two days prior. There was an occasion when the housekeeper had said that JonBenét was such a beautiful girl and asked Patsy if she was afraid that someone would kidnap her. Arndt relayed this information back to her bosses at the police station.

A trap is placed on the landline phone in the den to try and trace any incoming calls. Any outside calls could be made on Johns mobile phone (including those made by the police). Arndt watched as John answered every phone call and believes there were at least three times when the phone rang, and John has rushed into the den to answer it.

Sometime after 9am, John Fernie arrived back from the bank. The money had been arranged as the kidnapper had asked and was available as soon as John requested it. They wait. During this time Patsy remains unable to do or say anything. She is comforted by her friends, and Arndt is never able to take her to one side and ask some questions.

After 10am, Arndt speaks to John, who tells her that he had checked to see if all of the windows and the doors were locked that morning. It's strange that he fails to mention the open window in the basement, unless he goes to the basement later than what he originally said. The police suspect that maybe someone with a key could be linked to the kidnapping. John and Patsy tell Arndt that at least six people have a spare key to their house.

The forensic officer's show Arndt around the house. They have found no signs of any break in. Arndt stands on the landing and looks into JonBenét's bedroom. There is a pile of hair bands on the floor which look as if someone has thrown them. She then goes to the play area nearby. There is a life size doll that looks like JonBenét. It is the one she got for Christmas. It is naked. Although forensic officers have finished, JonBenét's bedroom is sealed. At 10.30am the officers begin to leave until Arndt is the only detective left. It is then that she realises John has also disappeared.

Patsy had spent most of the morning in the Sun Room, the room directly under the wine cellar, being comforted by friends. There were victim liaison officers who attended, but they never really got the chance to speak to Patsy or John due to the same friends acting as a barrier. Having been told by their bosses that the Ramseys were very important people and to treat them as victims, the police never gave John, Patsy, and their friends, any direct requests. They never asked the friends to leave, and they never asked John and Patsy any further questions about JonBenét.

In Johns office, Arndt did show John, Fleet and John Fernie, a copy of the ransom note. Both Fleet and John Fernie had ideas about what parts of the ransom note meant, but John remained silent. Arndt asked John about the specific sum of $118,000 but for some reason although John had named a few ex-employees who could be suspects, he does not mention that it's the same amount as his Christmas bonus and has been listed on his payslip since February. You would also think that *SBTC* would kick start something in John. He had been at the Subic Bay Training Centre in the sixties. The clear link was the word *Victory*, which John would have seen on the bank notes at the time.

Perhaps he was more interested in what were the FBI going to do when they turned up that afternoon. They were not bound to the notion of treating John and Patsy solely as victims. It's possible that they would have asked the friends to leave and then separated the Ramseys to get full accounts (before the body had been found). This could have been done away from the house, with John staying if the kidnappers rang. Aware that the FBI were on their way, one theory is that John had only sixty minutes left to discover the body. What he needed was an excuse to find it. Ironically, it was the FBI who were able to give it to him.

Chapter 7

The body is found.

Cover her face. Mine eyes dazzle. She died young.

John Webster, *The Duchess of Malfi.*

From the moment det. Linda Arndt called the station to say
that JonBenét's dead body had been found the basement of
her parent's house, those in charge had an important
decision to make. The FBI had been called because kidnaps
come under interstate offences. When it became a murder,
it fell solely under the jurisdiction of the Boulder Police
Department. The state of Colorado allowed police
departments to request assistance if needed. Along with the
gathering of evidence, there is an endless list of things that
remain hidden from the spotlight, but they still must be
done. For whatever reason the District Attorney's Office
and the chief of police in Boulder decided to go it alone.

Why? This is the same police department that has not
dealt with a murder all year, they don't even have a
homicide unit. This is the same police department with an
extremely liberal District Attorney's Office, preferring to

plea bargain rather than take a case to trial. The same D. A's office that would also be very close to the lawyers who would represent the Ramseys within hours of the body being found. But for some reason those in charge say they don't need the help of the FBI or any other officers from the state of Colorado. The only good news is that one FBI agent was on his way to the address when the call came in. The bad news was that he was told his services would be no longer required by the end of the day. Of all the mistakes made by Boulder police this was the most bizarre. It would not be the only mistake those in charge would make.

When John brings JonBenét up from the basement he has already touched the duct tape, the white blanket, JonBenét's clothing, and possibly a pink Barbie top found beside her. The boys long-johns she was wearing show that JonBenét had urinated while lying face down, but I don't know if they are soaking wet at this point. We should stop at this point and deal with the clothes she was wearing. Patsy never claimed she put a pair of boys long-johns on JonBenét the night before, nor some underwear that are twice the size of what JonBenét would normally have worn. She had told officer French that JonBenét was wearing long white underwear and a red turtleneck top when she was put into bed (although this account would later change). So, it is possible that Patsy believes JonBenét is still wearing those same clothes. Unfortunately, for some reason John has covered his dead child with a rug, and even gone as far as to use an old sweater to cover her legs.

Going back to the moment JonBenét is found, it is Fleet White who called out from the basement, come up the stairs and called out again for someone to ring for an ambulance. Meanwhile John has taken the duct tape off JonBenét's mouth and tried to loosen the cord around the wrists. He then removed JonBenét from the white blanket and carried the body up the narrow stairs. He has laid JonBenét down, spoke to Linda Arndt, and has then moved JonBenét into the living room where he has placed a rug and then a sweater over JonBenét. It is not until everyone has left the Sunroom that Patsy comes in from next door. Why she waited so long is a mystery.

As for DNA and fibres, Patsy was in the same clothes she was wearing when she had the Christmas party with the Whites (again) and all their guest. These are also the same clothes that have come into contact with the Stines (again), before Patsy hugs her dead child. Even with a rug and sweater thrown over the body, any defence team could argue that fibres and DNA from Patsy found on JonBenét could have come from the night before. Patsy tells the reverend that if Jesus could raise Lazarus, then he should be able to raise her daughter. The group then say a small prayer, although at no point has anyone mentioned how JonBenét died.

When the FBI and more detectives arrive about 1.30pm they finally decide to clear the scene. At this point one detective hears John speaking to his pilot about getting a plane to take him, Patsy, and Burke to Atlanta that afternoon. The simple explanation is that John is merely making arrangements to stay out of the house, although it does seem strange that this is one of the first things he thinks of, especially when the small foreign faction have still not got what they wanted. Around the same time John's two other children and his eldest daughter's boyfriend turn up. The police offer to put everyone up in a hotel (including the Whites and the Fernie's) to be able to get initial accounts and sort out seizing everyone's clothing. During all this confusion the Ramseys leave, saying they are going to stay at a friend's, with Patsy wearing the same clothes from the night before, and John wearing the clothes he had on when he found JonBenét in the basement. Unable to get a decision the police at the scene can only agree. Everyone is finally out by 2.45pm.

One of the fallouts from the Simpson trial is that even though the police are already in the house warrants must be in place. The police also leave, and now wait for a search warrant to be signed to be able to go back into the house to do another forensic search. For something that normally takes twenty minutes to complete, the District Attorney delays signing the warrant for six hours. JonBenét's body is still beside the Christmas tree. The police and a doctor finally go back in at 8.20pm. Of all the complaints against the police there are two positive things they have already done. They sealed off JonBenét's bedroom as soon as they could, and they also have a record of who went into the basement that morning. Officer French looks around the basement but does not open the wine cellar door, Fleet White looks around the basement and goes up to the broken window where he moves a piece of glass. He opens the wine cellar door but does not go in. John goes into the basement that morning, touches the suitcase, closes the broken window, but does not go into the wine cellar. A few hours later both John and Fleet go back down into the basement, both go again to up the broken window, and this time both go into the wine cellar. Once you have all these people's DNA and clothes, whatever's left would be of high importance. The only strange thing is that John still hasn't told police about the suitcase or the window. But to be fair, officers outside never mentioned the broken window either.

Was there no sign the weather grate had been recently moved, no sign of disturbance on the ground? I am not talking about footprints in the snow, its more about a person having to be as quiet as possible in the dark as they lifted the heavy grate, got down into the thin recess and then climbed through a small window. Silence would be more important than not leaving any marks. The easiest way would be to open the window fully, climb down, then sit and gently ease in legs first. But where are the signs that someone was here, where is the dirt on the basement carpet? Although, as yet, no one knows its relevance.

In Arndt's report she and another detective visit John after 9pm to see how the family are coping. John, who is staying at a friend's home, has his brother with him, who is an attorney. There is also his physician, who is also an attorney. He finally mentions the paradox of the suitcase under the broken window. How different things would have been if he had mentioned it sometime after 6am. Why he has waited so long could be explained that he was more interested in getting his daughter back; but if it was important enough to tell police that night it was probably more important when the forensic officers were at the house that morning. It now means the police must go get another warrant and carry out a third search of the home.

The police ask about Patsy's welfare. One lawyer tells them that they cannot speak to Patsy as she has taken medication. When asked when John and Patsy can give an interview to try and find out more about who killed their daughter, John's physician tells police that Patsy may be unable to do this due to her fragile status. John's reply was to give them two days. It was left for the Ramseys to contact police as to when they wished to give as much information as they could about the circumstances leading up to their daughter's death. Although they did not realise it, the police were in for a long wait. But one person who lived in the house was spoken to on this day.

Detective Patterson went and spoke to Burke that afternoon while he was at Fleet White's house. An adult was present, but it was not a member of Burke's family or a parental guardian. John and Patsy never gave permission for Burke to be spoken to by police. As such, what was said in that conversation was blocked from being used in any court. Perhaps the best information would come from the other child, the one who would remain silent forever, but JonBenét could also be the police's best witness in helping to solve this crime.

After the body had been found the police went straight to the District Attorney's office that afternoon to get a search warrant. It was finally signed at 8pm. After being taken to the address the waiting doctor was the first person to enter the house at 8.23pm. JonBenét had remained all this time by the Christmas tree. The white cord was still around her neck, one end tied to a broken artists paintbrush. The doctor noted that petechial haemorrhaging, blood spots in the eyes, could be seen, indicating that death had been caused by strangulation, or more precisely, lack of air reaching the lungs. The time of death was not noted. Witnesses had reported JonBenét was in a high state of rigour mortis when she was found at 1pm. As this starts around twelve hours after death, she could have been killed anytime between 10.30pm and 1am but unlikely to have happened sometime after. Her temperature was not taken, possibly due to being moved from the cold wine cellar to the warm living room six hours ago. The marks on the side of her face were noted. In the room by the Christmas tree the doctor noted there were no other obvious signs of trauma.

By the time the child's body was taken away, neighbours and a few reporters were waiting outside. Amid the red and white candy canes were ribbons of yellow and black police *Do Not Cross* tape strewn between the trees.

The police at the scene were then told the basement window. They took some photographs that night but would have to get another warrant to search again in the morning. This would lead to an issue of whether a spider's web could have been spun in the window frame within the last twenty-four hours; or that no one came in or out of the window in the last few months.

But the police had made some significant finds on that first day. A black Maglite flashlight, big enough to hold three large batteries, had been standing upright on the kitchen unit all this time. A bowl of pineapple pieces and a glass of iced tea had been left on the table in the breakfast room, although no one had eaten it that day. The police already had the pad the ransom note was written in, even if they didn't know it. When they went back into the house on a further search, they would also find the Sharpie pen that had been used to write the note. With the broken paintbrush used for the garotte, they found one end in the basement in Patsy's paint tray even though the tip was missing. They had the piece of duct tape which had been put over JonBenet's mouth. It was ripped at both ends, meaning it had come from a roll that had been used before, but no roll was found in the house. The white cord used to tie JonBenét's wrists and around her neck was new, but again none was found in the house. The red turtleneck top that

JonBenét had not worn to the Christmas party, and so presumably was put on her when she was asleep, was later found scrunched up in JonBenét's bathroom. As for the white pyjamas she was put to bed in, I don't believe Patsy would have used a pair of boys well-worn long-johns, so I would list the original bottoms as missing as well. JonBenét had also been found wearing a new pair of size 12 panties, clearly too large for her and not what Patsy would have put on her daughter that night. These would be significant when the post-mortem was held the next day.

Chapter 8

Timeline of Events.

How heavily it dies

    Into the west away;

Past touch and sight and sound

Not further to be found,

How hopeless under ground

    Falls the remorseful day.

    A. E. Housman, *How Clear, How Lovely Bright.*

Some of the dates and times have been taken from various sources.

Summer 1996. John returns home at night and realises he does not have his keys. Patsy and the children are away. John removes the weather grate and kicks in a glass pane in one of the basement windows. He then takes of his suit and just in his boxer shorts he climbs down into the recess and drops down into the basement through the window.

15th November. Surprise party for Patsy at the house. Approx hundred people attend. Possible catering team at address.

Thanksgiving week. The housekeepers husband cleans all the windows at the house.

7th December. Birthday party for John at the house. Numerous guests from both Johns company and social life. Approx hundred people.

Two weeks before Christmas, the housekeeper Linda Hoffman, along with her husband, her adult daughters, and their partners, were at address to help put up Christmas decorations. This included going down into the wine cellar in the basement to get out the Christmas trees.

13th December. Party at the house. Approx sixty people.

17th December. JonBenét crowned as Little Miss Christmas.

21st December. The local paper has article on John, as his company Access Graphics, celebrates 1 billion dollars turnover that year. It also mentions the company's links to Lockheed Martin, one of the largest military suppliers in the world.

22nd December. JonBenét appears in the mall to sing Rocking Around the Christmas Tree. She later appears in the Christmas parade as Little Miss Colorado. The parade float includes her name on the side.

23rd December. Party at the house. Approx sixty guests, plus children and catering staff.

24th December. The family goes out for a meal, then drive around to look at the Christmas lights. When the children are in bed John goes over to a neighbour's house to collect JonBenét's bike.

Christmas day.
6am. Burke gets up first. He wakes JonBenét. Both go up to the top floor and their parents' bedroom. Patsy goes downstairs in pyjamas and no make-up. Some photographs are taken. JonBenét gets a life-size doll that looks exactly like her and is wearing her clothes.
12pm. When interviewed four months later and asked about the lack of luggage for the holiday, John said he took some luggage and Christmas presents to the airport on Christmas day. They didn't need that much luggage as they already had clothes at their holiday home.

Afternoon. Other children from the neighbourhood come over. JonBenét plays outside on her bike.

5pm. Ramseys get ready to go to Fleet White's home 10 minutes' drive away. JonBenét refuses to wear the same items of clothing as Patsy (red top, black velvet pants). She wears the white top she is later found in and a pair of black pants.

5.30pm. Party at Fleet White's house. Among the guests are other children.

8.30 – 9.30pm. The Ramseys leave Fleet Whites house. They make two stops for Patsy to drop off presents. It is not known how long this takes or if JonBenét was awake for either.

9.30-10.30pm. Jonbenet falls asleep in the car and is carried up to her bedroom by John. Her black pants are changed by Patsy, but she leaves the white top on. Everyone in the family claims they were asleep by 10.30pm.

Midnight. A neighbour looks over and believes the Ramseys kitchen light is on.

26th December.
1 - 2am. A neighbour hears a scream. Two years later the neighbour would change her account and believes the scream was two nights before Christmas. Another

neighbour believes they hear something metal landing on concrete.

5.30am. John gets up first to take a shave and a shower. Patsy gets up, gets dressed in the same clothes she had on the night before, puts on her makeup, and goes downstairs while John is still in the shower. She stops by the laundry area to wash an item of JonBenét's clothing. She goes down the spiral staircase and sees the ransom note. She goes back up, realises JonBenet is missing from her bed, goes and looks in Burke's bedroom, and then calls for John, who comes down a set of stairs (unknown which one). It is still dark outside.

5.52am – Patsy calls police. After telling the operator that her daughter has gone, she hangs up. The controller keeps the line open and believes she hears possibly three people speaking.

5.54am. Patsy calls her friends.

5.59am. The first police officers arrive on scene. John and Patsy take officer French through the house to show the three pages of ransom notes on the floor, but do not touch it. Officer French looks around the basement for any signs of a break-in. He sees the wooden latch in the top corner of the wine cellar door. As he is looking for the kidnappers escape route, he does not open door. The police have been informed to treat the Ramseys with deference, and for strict radio silence. Officer French does not give details of the ransom note over the radio, instead, an officer leaves the scene to take it to the police station.

6 – 7am. Fleet and Priscilla White, along with John and Priscilla Fernie, arrive at the address. Fleet White searches basement. He opens wine cellar door but sees nothing.

7am. Burke is taken out of the house by Fleet White and John Fernie. They return about 7.45am. In the meantime reverend Hoverstock arrives.

Sometime between 7-11am. John searches the basement. He sees the broken window is open and closes it. The wide time difference is because John gave different times during different interviews.

8.10am. Detective Linda Arndt arrives with a wire trap and a photocopy of the ransom note. She finds Priscilla and Fleet White, Barbara and John Fernie, and reverend Hoverstock. She is told John Fernie and Fleet had taken Burke out of the house. Arndt has a pager, but it can only bleep when someone wishes to contact her. John Ramsey lets her use his mobile phone to call the station. John

Fernie goes to the bank to sort out getting the ransom money.

8-10am. Police wait for the telephone call, it never happens. Arndt shows a copy of the ransom note to John, he does not comment about the link between the ransom demand and his Christmas bonus. At 10am neither John nor Patsy asks what is going on or what is going to happen next.

Around 10.30am. Forensic officers complete their search of the bedroom, the spiral staircase, and the ground floor doors and windows. The police tell John they are going to leave to have a debrief at the station with the FBI. Det. Arndt is now the only officer in the house, trying to deal with seven people.

10.30- 10.45am. Arndt notices that John Ramsey has disappeared.

10.30 - 11am. FBI agent Ron Walker arrives at Boulder police station. The 10am deadline has come and gone. Walker looks at the ransom note. He believes this is a staged note and that it may not be a kidnap.

11.45am. There is limited communication with Arndt at the address. She informs the FBI that there has so far been no call from the kidnappers, and that John Ramsey has been missing for about an hour.

12.30pm. John comes back to where Arndt has been staying by the phone in the den. Arndt informs the police station that John has returned. She is told by the FBI to keep him busy until they arrive, and to keep an eye on him.

1pm. Arndt tells John about checking the house from top to bottom. He and Fleet White go immediately to the basement.

1.02pm John Ramsey finds JonBenét's body. Fleet White runs up the stairs shouting for someone to call an ambulance. John comes up the stairs with the body and places it on a rug in the hallway.

1.05pm. Det Arndt moves the body and places it beside Christmas Tree in the main room. John places a rug over the body to cover her neck, and then a sweater to cover the lower legs and feet. It is only now that Pasty comes out of the sunroom and sees that her daughter is dead.

1.20pm. FBI agent Ron Walker arrives at crime scene.

1.40pm. John makes a phone call to a pilot about taking a private plane to Atlanta. Police tell him that he and his family to stay.

1.44pm. Johns other children, John-Andrew and Melinda arrive. Everyone begins to leave.

2.30pm. John and Patsy leave without a police officer in attendance. Rather than stay in a hotel, they stay with friends and within the hour contact separate attorneys for both John and Patsy. Police request a search warrant.

8pm. Police finally get a search warrant signed to re-enter the house. It is now dark outside.

8.23pm. The coroner attends and checks the body of JonBenét. His initial diagnosis at the scene is that JonBenét died of strangulation. He does not give a time of death.

10pm.The body is removed.

Part Two.

Bitter Harvest.

Chapter 9

Words & Actions.

Crime is common. Logic is rare. Therefore, it is upon the logic rather than upon the crime that you should dwell.

Sir Arthur Conan Doyle, *The Copper Beeches*.

The next morning a briefing was held at the police station. There would have been four things that every officer would want to know:

What was the time of death? Narrowing that down would eliminate a lot of suspects if they had a rock-solid alibi. It would also mean police could focus their questioning when speaking to people.

How did she die? Officers would have known about the ligature, but what sort of knot was it, where had the cord come from. Working with the first question you can then circle around what must have happened before and after the death. This would include how did she get to the basement, and how did the kidnapper get out?

What's the best evidence? The kidnapper had left a series of clues in the ransom note. They certainly seemed to know a lot about John, and the house. But they had also made some bizarre decisions. Why did they leave JonBenét in the house when they could have still got the money?

The last question is usually a management issue: How many resources do we have? You had a number of people named by the Ramsey's. For every one let's say you needed two detectives to investigate until they were eliminated. It may have been at this point that another line of enquiry would need to be looked at, the parents themselves. As well as treating the family as victims, you also need to create a separate team to treat them as suspects. The answer would be to get them interviewed as soon as possible to either charge or rule them out. We have not even included the officers required for general enquiries, CCTV, house to house, dealing with information that comes in from the public. What may have come as a shock to detectives around the table that morning was the bosses declining the help of the FBI and forces from other states to try and solve this case. It might have been pride. The media had become interested, and it seemed to be a bigger news story every hour. Local journalists had been joined by national news presenters and magazine reporters. There were even people on this new thing called the internet. The decision to keep it in Boulder may have also been political. Out of state help requires the authority of the Governor of Colorado. By keeping the investigation local the District Attorney's office would have the final say on how the investigation would continue. Detectives may have pissed and moaned; but there would have been another question asked around the table: What do you think happened?

Any initial investigation is like trying to complete a jigsaw puzzle but only being able to see certain parts of the picture. You can start to link the pieces of evidence together and see if they fit. The problem is whether everyone is looking at the same thing. Coming in with a different point of view could lead you to miss the details. The ransom note implied an intruder. A child killed at home usually points to someone in the family. Most child abductions happen during the day. JonBenét was taken some time between 11pm and 1am. It already felt as though there were two distinct images trying to pull the investigation out of focus. The detectives knew that at least the evidence doesn't care about emotions, it doesn't care about politics, and it doesn't care about what particular stories you wish to believe. Evidence is there to shine a light on facts. But when police received the autopsy report, the picture suddenly became darker.

The initial autopsy was completed that morning. It would take a few weeks for the full report, which would include toxicology, brain scans and stomach contents to become available. The pathologist described her as a *"Well-nourished Caucasian female, body measures 47 inches in length, and weighs an estimated 45 pounds. The scalp is covered by long blonde hair, which is fixed in two ponytails, one on top of the head secured by a cloth hair tie and blue elastic band, and one in the lower back of the head secured by a blue elastic band."*

But the next sentence gave a new perspective as to what had gone on in the house. *"Cause of death of this six-year-old female is asphyxia by strangulation associated with craniocerebral trauma"*. The words did not adequately describe the full details of the skull injury. JonBenét had a large 8-inch fracture running along the top right of her skull. Part of it had been crushed by the impact of a rounded blunt instrument. The report did state that there was no major skeletal damage to the neck, which ruled out the injury being caused by JonBenét having a fall of some kind. For the police who had seen the body at the house it was a shock. There was no blood. Even stranger, the pathologist believed the skull fracture could have occurred at least ninety minutes before she had been strangled. The initial examination put her dying between 11pm of the 25th and 1am of the 26th; with the widest time limit being 10pm to 2am. JonBenét had been in advanced rigor mortis when she was found at 1pm on the 26th. If she had been assaulted by the kidnapper at 11pm, why didn't the parents hear anything. And if it was a kidnapper, did they then stay in the house for over an hour before killing her?

Then there was the strangulation itself. Another shock. The pathologist report stated there were no internal ruptures in the neck that indicated force had been used. Although she had died of strangulation, it was quite possible her breathing had become so shallow due to the head injury that even the slightest pressure on her throat would have been enough to stop air getting into her lungs. Detectives must have wondered why anyone would create a garotte when it clearly wasn't needed, and it clearly had not been used. The reason the garotte looked so horrific in the autopsy photos was because all the muscles in the neck collapsed after JonBenét had died, making it look as if it was embedded into her skin. The cord had been wrapped twice, and were lateral, indicating she had not struggled when it was placed around her neck. It could also mean that it was put on by someone the same height as JonBenét, or that she had been lying face down and someone had been standing over her. Once the cords around her neck had been removed, the pathologist saw other abrasions. There was a mark to the left of her neck which had bruised, meaning it had been caused up to an hour before she died. There was also a mark on the right side of her neck just above the furrow caused by the cord. Located under the right side of her chin was a small abrasion. This could indicate that a person has used their left-hand to grab JonBenét by the throat while she was still conscious.

There were other marks on her body which also indicated that some sort of struggle might have taken place earlier that night. There were two rust-colored abrasions on the right side of her face, and an almost identical set on her back. The coroner, viewing the body less than 48hrs after death, put these as abrasions, meaning superficial injuries to the skin, not burn marks. There is no mention that the skin was punctured or that there was blood around these marks.

The coroner noted that JonBenét was wearing a long sleeve white top with a star on the front. There is no report of any blood stains on it. She was also wearing well-used boys (it had a fly at the front) white long-johns which were stained with urine. Underneath these JonBenét wore white panties with rosebuds on them and the word "Wednesday" on the front band. The panties were also urine stained at the front. Inside the crotch area the pathologist saw "Several red areas of staining". They were not going to say if it was blood until the full autopsy report. We should also say that the pathologist did not state if JonBenét had urinated before or after she had died, but as the stains were at the front in a circular shape, we can assume she was lying face down when it happened.

JonBenét had been washed and cleaned around her thighs, and her genital area showed signs of chronic inflammation. This could be due to the possibility of being cleaned with a chemical detergent, or her ongoing bedwetting issues.   The police still had the issue that these were not the clothes Patsy said she had put JonBenét to bed in. She was to later change her mind about the red turtleneck and say she kept her in the white top, but she never gave a definitive answer to the underwear and long-johns. If detectives wondered why the kidnapper had put

JonBenét into a different outfit before (or even possibly after) she died, the next part of the autopsy report may have held the answer.

It could also be possible signs of a sexual trauma (which could have been caused by JonBenét herself). There were a few tiny spots of blood found in the underwear, but it was not clear if this had been caused post death. There were also very small abrasions in the vagina consistent with some type of trauma, and watery fluid, which would later turn out not to be semen, but possibly the result of being cleaned (is she now lying on her back?). The upper vagina contained no sign of any abnormalities, although there were signs of chronic inflammation consistent with long term bedwetting/vaginitis. Again, the coroner could not say what happened to her, but there were detectives who believed some sort of digital penetration had occurred. There were nearly forty registered sex offenders within a two-mile radius of the Ramsey's home, and they were just the ones the police had convicted. More enquiries that needed to be made, but no extra resources to be made available. The autopsy report still wasn't finished.

The pathologist noted that JonBenét had "*yellow to light green-tan apparent vegetable or fruit material which may represent fragments of pineapple.*" There is no mention of anything else in her stomach. It takes between thirty minutes to two hours for food to pass through the stomach to the small intestine. This means JonBenét ate this one thing possibly an hour before she died. As well as the ransom note being one of the strangest in history, the autopsy report for what had been classified as a murder was also turning out to be one of the strangest in history. A child seemingly strangled to death, in fact died after receiving a head injury and her vital organs broke down. There was inflammation/trauma around the vaginal area, but then someone took the time to clean her. This was a kidnapping, but somebody left the body behind. She had been asleep when she got home on Christmas night and carried her into bed. Then somebody had woken her up and given her something to eat?

Somebody remembered that in the house yesterday morning was a bowl of pineapple pieces on the breakfast table. If JonBenét had gone straight up to bed on Christmas night, and John and Patsy had been dealing with the kidnap from the moment they woke up, and Burke had been ushered out of the house straight from his bedroom, when did someone find the time to eat? The forensic officers then informed detectives that the bowl had Patsy and Burke's fingerprints on it (I don't know if there were any smudge marks consistent with someone wearing gloves handling the bowl). The glass of iced tea next to the bowl only contained Burke's fingerprints.

The pathologist noted that fingernail clippings were taken, and as standard policy the family were verbally informed of the autopsy results soon after it had been completed. I am not sure if they would have been told about any sexual trauma, but they would be able to have a copy of the report once it had been typed. I also don't know if the pineapple in the stomach was mentioned as it was not linked to her death. The pathologist had no way of knowing what the parents had said about when they got home, nor would the pathologist know about the bowl of pineapple on the breakfast table.

In some ways, detectives were worse off now than before they had sat down for their briefing. The time of death was a four-hour window of between 10pm and 2am. The best they could get was possibly between 11pm and 1am, with midnight being the witching hour. That's still a large window when the suspect is still unknown, and it could have been someone who had got in through a small basement window. As for the cause of death, this was also now up for debate. What appeared to be a strangulation now included a skull injury, an assault, and sexual trauma, some of these possibly happening an hour before she was killed, possibly at the time of death, possibly after she had died. And now the pathologist was telling them that JonBenét had eaten a piece of pineapple that night. But how could that be if JonBenét was put to bed by her parents straight after they got back from the party? Again, the family were key in obtaining detailed accounts of who might have been involved in the kidnapping. The police would also be fully aware that with any child homicide the parents are the first people that need to be eliminated. To do that they should have been treated as possible suspects at the very start. The defence team in the O.J. Simpson trial kept repeating to the jury that Simpson was treated as a suspect because he was black. The Boulder District Attorney repeatedly told the police both John and Patsy were to be treated as victims because they were rich. Any change in the narrative was bound to cause friction. The police would have to tell them they were suspects.

This should be quite normal. You say to the parents they are going to be investigated first in order to be eliminated first; but there were two underlying issues. One was how quickly the Ramseys obtained a legal team. Even if other people were saying you should get legal advice (although it seems very strange that this sort of conversation would happen so soon), surely you would be wanting to speak to the police just to find out what they were doing to catch your daughters' killer? There is also another anomaly in that there were two Ramsey Defence Teams, one for John, and one for Patsy. This is very expensive and time-consuming, and usually only happens when there could be a possible conflict of interest between two suspects, as in one person's story may somehow implicate the other. But the Ramseys were rich enough to hire the best defence lawyers in Boulder, some of whom were very close to staff working in the District Attorney's office.

For detectives who suspected the Ramseys knew more than what they had originally said, the best thing to do would be to bring them in as quickly as possible to get their accounts. Once they had been eliminated the police could look at the outer circle of family and friends, plus people who had regularly attended the house in the last few months. Again, a young child is not like a young adult who may have a secret world their parents know nothing about; this would be a relatively simple case of going through the list until it narrows. The police even had a major piece of evidence, the ransom note.

The longest kidnap note in American history had mentioned John's business, which implied it could be someone linked to his company. The note demanded a small amount of ransom money, and Patsy had told them the housekeeper had also asked for a small amount of money. The housekeeper could have seen one of John's pay slips and so believed he had that amount in his bank. How many of us have been to a friend's home and know every room, or would be comfortable to move around in the dark? The ransom note links the writer to someone who had been inside that address on numerous occasions. The Ramsey's needed to be interviewed as soon as possible.

I should mention that the word "Interview" in this sense is not a suspect interview; it is a "significant witness" interview, with police officers trained to go into specific details about things they believe are important to the investigation. Detectives looked to the D.A. to make a decision as to whether to bring the Ramseys in or wait for them to do a voluntary interview. The D.A. remembered the Simpson fiasco and decided to ask the Ramsey's to come in when they were ready. The D.A knew they would be sued for millions if there was no evidence to arrest. They were willing to wait for the possibility of DNA results to find the suspect. How long they were willing to wait would be a contentious issue. It still felt as though no one was really in charge.

The Ramseys informed the police they were going to bury their child in Atlanta within the week and would let them know when they would give an interview. This was another shock. Due to so many strange circumstances in relation to the autopsy, the police would often request a second autopsy to be done to resolve issues which may be contested in court. Now, not only was their silent witness going to be buried in a few days; but the main witnesses were going to remain silent until then. As such, detectives were left working on two narratives, trying to see two different pictures, one from outside the house, the other from inside. When the pathologist had put in his report that there were almost two causes of death, the police must have been wondering if the killer also had more than one face?

Chapter 10

Home Alone.

Alibi: the plea of having been at the time of the commission of an act elsewhere than at the place of commission.

Webster's Dictionary.

One narrative that seems to crop up on a regular basis is that the police allowed much of the evidence to be compromised and even possibly destroyed by not clearing the house of people. But I would argue most of the evidence was captured within the first two hours of police arriving, and the rest of it was captured after the body was found and everyone had left. JonBenét's bedroom was only entered that morning by Patsy and the forensic team. If the white blanket found with JonBenét came from the laundry area, then we know only Patsy and the kidnapper went there. We know that the kidnapper used the spiral staircase, as did Patsy and possibly John. We know the kidnapper went to the desk under the wall phone to take a pad and pen, as did Patsy to use the phone, and John when he handed over notepads to the police. All those crime scenes had already been flawed to some degree because John and Patsy lived there, but whatever forensic evidence was left would be the kidnappers. The same is true when this turns into a murder investigation. If we believe the intruder came in and out through the basement window, we also know who had gone down there that morning.

There is the story that people were cleaning up during that morning; but what does this mean, somebody gave the kitchen a wipe? We know friends arrived to comfort Patsy, but it's not clear what else they do as their statements have never been released to the public. Victim advocates are in the house to also comfort the family, and its believed at some point they go out to get food, but we don't know how much clearing up they did afterwards. What we do know is that by 10am the forensic officers had finished examining the parts of the house that the kidnapper may have been in. It is also worth mentioning that neither John nor Patsy ever pointed out a large black flashlight standing upright on the kitchen unit. One, because they never officially claimed to be theirs. Two, even if it was theirs, did they leave it their overnight? We also have the bowl of pineapple in the breakfast room. If people really were going around cleaning up, wouldn't they have washed the bowl and glass? The answer is probably no one cleaned up, and no one checked the breakfast room to see if anything was out of place. If there was a kidnapper, would they have given JonBenét a piece of pineapple from the bowl and left it there? But both items had been left without being touched. And when everyone had left on the afternoon of the 26th, police could finally have a good look around the house.

The master bedroom on the top floor seems to have been left alone by police that morning. This would be a reasonable reaction to what was believed to be a kidnapping. Everyone would have been looking for the entry and exit point on the ground floor. I don't even know if the bedroom was ever forensically examined afterwards. John and Patsy (and possibly Burke) left with some of the items they had been wearing the night before. They would have been told the house would be a crime scene for a couple for days, so no doubt they would have also taken some luggage with them. I don't know if this was searched either. Patsy would later ask her sister to collect numerous items before JonBenét's funeral. John and Patsy never went back to the house again.

The master bedroom has a fireplace, two changing areas, two bathrooms (allegedly Patsy's shower was not working the morning after Christmas day), and two staircases. The staircase nearest Patsy's bed goes down to the front of the house to Burkes bedroom. If you were to use that staircase you would then need to walk along the length of the house to reach JonBenet's bedroom, going past a large open play area. You can see the life size doll that JonBenét got for Christmas. Patsy gave the toy maker her daughters vital statistics, and some of JonBenét's outfits, although for some reason the doll is not wearing any clothes. There are also two spare bedrooms, one of which Patsy used as a treatment room when she was suffering from cancer, which now has an open suitcase on the bed. Next to JonBenét's bedroom is a laundry area which included a washing machine and a tumble dryer. It is believed the white blanket found in the wine cellar came from here. Police noted there was an open bag of pull up diapers hanging out of laundry a cupboard that morning.

I don't know if Burke's room was searched by the police or checked for fingerprints on that day. Why should they when it was a kidnapper who had broken in and taken JonBenét. The police had been told by their bosses to treat the Ramseys with respect and this would have included Burke, which was probably the reason he was allowed to leave before anyone could even ask if he saw or heard anything in the night. The crime scene photographs show two beds in Burke's room. Whether this was for sleepovers, or that he also had a bedwetting problem like JonBenét, I don't know. In relation to clothes, there doesn't appear to be any lying around. You would think a nine-year-old would have the clothes he wore Christmas morning, the clothes he wore for the Christmas party, his pyjamas, and perhaps even what he was going to be wearing for the flight to Michigan left on the floor. But for some reason this young boy has the tidiest room in the whole house. I have no idea if the clothes he was wearing the night before were ever seized. John and Patsy did not give the police the clothes they wore on Christmas night until over a year later.

How much relevant forensic evidence was taken from JonBenét's bedroom has never been disclosed. Looking for clues in a kidnap is different than looking for evidence in a murder. That morning it was believed someone had come in and carried her away in the quickest amount of time they could. With a murder you now have the possibility that events could have started in the bedroom or if the room showed signs of having been recently cleaned. We must also accept that if forensic officers had entered the bedroom for the first time knowing it was a murder, they might have started with the presumption that the clothes she was found in might not have been the clothes she had died in, and so treated every other item of clothing as evidence. The shoes and black pants JonBenét wore to the Christmas party were found crumpled on the floor near the door, although it is not clear if there was any underwear inside. The same is true with the bed. We must assume a waterproof liner was on the mattress due to previous bedwetting issues, but we don't know if the bed sheets had been freshly laundered or contained clothing fibres.

We know that Patsy and John say they were in the bedroom the night before and helped put the sleeping JonBenét to bed. That morning Patsy did not run to the en-suite bathroom or looked under the beds or opened wardrobes to check for her daughter, so it's possible any mess was caused by the intruder. This bedroom also has a balcony, so it's strange neither John nor Patsy go to the balcony doors to check what may have been the kidnappers most obvious escape route. The room is sealed after crime scene officers are finished that morning, so at least a forensic team can go back into a sterile environment when it becomes a murder investigation. If we stick with the kidnapper theory, how does someone who may have left DNA on the long johns and panties that JonBenét was wearing when she was found, and who may have left their DNA under her fingernails, not leave any in her bedroom?

Patsy says she walked past JonBenét's bedroom that morning, noticing the door was slightly open, just how she had left it (why would someone carrying a child close the door to how it had been?) and goes to the laundry area. Here she washes an item of JonBenét's clothing in the sink. It is approx. 5.30am, Patsy is fully dressed and wearing make-up, and presumably has turned a light on. Next to the sink is a tumble dryer. It's believed the white blanket was taken from the tumble dryer and somehow ended up with JonBenét in the wine cellar. Also in the wine cellar was a pink Barbie top. This was JonBenét's favourite thing and usually kept it on her bed. One theory is that it was also in the tumble dryer and stuck to the white blanket by static. There are four spots of blood on the front of the top, so if it had been recently cleaned, how did the blood get there?

Police photographs of the spare room show a double bed. On it is an open suitcase and items of clothing at the side. Did Patsy stop halfway through packing? I cannot tell who these clothes belong to, or which holiday they are for, the trip to Michigan or the Florida cruise. Just like JonBenét's bedroom there are also items on the floor. It is not clear if they had been dropped or thrown. Later, a bag containing a length of rope was recovered. About two years after their daughter's death John and Patsy were asked about the rope. They claimed they had absolutely no knowledge of it. Around the same time Lou Smit, a former detective and now a private investigator working for the

Ramsey Defence Team, put forward the theory that the ransom note was written before JonBenét had been killed and that the intruder had hidden under the bed of this room. Again, a criminal mastermind who somehow leaves part of his kidnapping kit behind does not make sense.

We go down the spiral staircase. It is very narrow and would be extremely difficult to manoeuvre in the dark. There is only one banister that runs on the outside. Although the risers stay the same height, the steps triangulate out from one inch to possibly fifteen inches. Patsy said she stepped over the ransom note on the way down; but she would have found it extremely difficult to step over it on the way back up. In the first set of police photographs there is a bin bag of old clothes at the bottom of the spiral staircase. I don't know if they were the Ramseys old clothes, items they were taking to Michigan, or perhaps a bag of clothes a neighbour had dropped off for Patsy to give away. Patsy would later tell police the bag was filled with clothes they were taking on holiday. This area of the hallway opens out to a series of doors, one to the garage, one to the study, another to the kitchen, and another to the breakfast room. There is also a gap in the wall which leads to the butler's pantry.

Staying by the spiral staircase, nearby was a desk and a telephone on the wall. The desk contained the writing pad used for the ransom note. On top of the desk was a dish filled with pens, one of which was the Sharpie pen used to write the note. This means an intruder has looked through the desk for a writing pad, has taken a pen, gone somewhere in the house, written the three-page note (after a couple of practice notes), returned the notepad and pen where they had come from, then left the ransom note on the stairs. We would also have to say this was all done in the dark…possibly.

Moving to the kitchen we have the flashlight that no one admits to owning, and in the breakfast room we have a bowl of pineapple pieces with Patsy and Burke's fingerprints on them that no one remembers putting out. There is a fireplace in the living room with the largest of the ten Christmas trees in the house. There are thirteen doors on the ground floor, including the one for the basement. Seven of these doors lead to the outside. There are at least twelve windows that someone could have opened.

In the basement you have a bathroom to your left, and the boiler room in the front. From photos and video footage the basement appeared to be filled with clutter. If anything was to go wrong, such as a power cut, the basement would be where you would go into the darkness to fix it, but you would need a flashlight to do so. There is a window in the boiler room area, although it is too small for anyone to get in and out. I believe there may have been an old furnace here, although I don't know if it was working or what type of fuel it used. At the end was a door to which was going to be the wine cellar at some point in the future. But like every other room in the basement, it seemed to be a place where John and Patsy stored things they did not want others to see, and at the same time did not want to throw them away.

This white painted door was locked by a white painted wooden latch nailed into the white doorframe. First, you had to know it was there, and then you had to reach up 6 feet six inches to twist the block of wood around to open the door. A kidnapper must have turned this latch twice. But why would they lock that door if it made no difference to their escape, nor does it make any difference to someone eventually finding the body? You had the possibility that the police would search the whole house as soon as they arrived, and it is only by an officer believing that the kidnapper could not have escaped through the white door that it wasn't.

The room itself is not carpeted. It contains wrapped presents that someone has partially opened. The wrapping was the same as the presents that Burke and JonBenét's presents had been wrapped in on Christmas day. Who were these presents for, and who may have tried to open them to see what was inside? John had told police he had gone to the aerodrome on Christmas day to pack the plane with some presents, so it's possible the ones in the wine cellar might have been birthday presents for Burke. It's also possible one of these presents was the large sized underwear that JonBenét was found wearing. There are two partial shoe marks on the floor. One *Hi-Tec*, the other belonging to the *SAS* brand. Burke had a pair of Hi-Tec boots, and SAS shoes were an expensive brand at the time. What I don't know is when and how these marks were formed. The floor was bare concrete with various building materials such as paint tubs lying around. It could be that a powder had been stepped on and had then set, so these marks may be many months old.

Moving out from the wine cellar and back into the boiler room, there is a bag of golf clubs, an artist's paint tray and tins of paint. Next to them is a stain on the carpet which is believed to be urine. This is possibly where JonBenét died. The urine stains on the underwear and long-johns, and the way the garotte is looped at the back of her neck indicates that she was lying face down when she was strangled. Of all the things that John asked his sister-in-law to collect from the house within three days of his daughter's death, he wanted that set of golf clubs. We then go back out and turn left into what appears to be a workstation area.

Nearby are more bin bags filled with of old clothes. A pair of scissors lie on a desk where Christmas decorations and presents were made and wrapped. There is a door to another laundry room, and beyond that a door to another room used as storage space. If the wine cellar was filled with old building materials, this room is more personal. Piled all over the floor appears to be old office equipment and paperwork, relics of John and Patsy's past. We move out and head towards the largest room in the basement.

The games room was rectangular shaped with a section that jutted out where an elevator used to be, now the shaft was used for storage space. There are a couple of movie posters on the wall. One is for Agatha *Christie's Death on the Nile* (1978 version). This is a film in which one crime is faked to commit another more serious crime; where items that should be at the scene have somehow disappeared, forged documents are part of the investigation, and people are willing to do anything for love. The female suspect also dies before justice can be reached. The focal point of the games room is a large green baize table with a model train set on it. As with nearly all of the other rooms there are various items on the floor, such as pieces of train tracks. There are books and toys on shelves next to a white footstool. Moving past a red chair we come up to the broken window with the suitcase under it.

Outside, the heavy weather grate was hinged to the wall. It appears to not be able to stand upright by itself. This meant that when you lifted it up you had to keep holding it up. John Ramsey was to say later that when he climbed through the window, he took the whole grate off. This enabled him to climb down into the narrow space, smash out a windowpane (from the pictures he doesn't even remove the jagged shards stuck in the frame), and reach in to unlock and turn the handle without cutting himself. He then had to push the window open. At this point we should note that the window opens inwards, but not fully, as it is stopped by pipes in the ceiling. In the narrow recess John would have to manoeuvre his body to slide through the gap feet first onto the basement floor. And he did all this just in a pair of boxer shorts.

The scene is flawed somewhat by Fleet White. He stated that when he first went into the basement he moved the suitcase slightly and saw some pieces of glass on the carpet. He put these on the windowsill. As the window opens inwards, there is no sill in the basement, so we must assume that the window was open at the time and Fleet has put the pieces of glass outside in the recess area. He cannot remember closing the window, which matches John's account of when he first checks the basement and sees the window open.

Police video footage of the blue suitcase shows a fragment of glass resting near the handle. The idea of a piece of glass falling from a height of at least three feet, landing on the case about ten inches wide, presumably bouncing and then stopping on the case, is hard to believe. If you go through the scenario logically, the intruder must have used the basement window to enter, because if they had used another way, such as a ground floor window, then they would have left the same way. Surely any loose fragment of glass that had been on the windowsill or in the window itself would have fallen then. To get out, the intruder places the suitcase under the window, which we must assume has been left open. Are we saying that while crouched down in the narrow confines of the recess as they were escaping they stopped to close the window, and a fragment of glass falls onto the case then? This leaves us with two options: The glass fragment on the suitcase under the open window is staging, a breadcrumb to lead the police away from what really happened. Or the intruder has stepped on the fragment and then when they have stood on the suitcase it has come loose and remained in situ. This is certainly possible, but again, let's look at the bigger picture. The first is that Patsy claimed she had picked all the glass up months ago. How did she miss any? The second is that I don't know if John or Patsy or even the cleaner ever said where the suitcase had been placed originally, but even if it had always been kept in the games room, why anyone would use a suitcase rather than the red chair or the footstool to stand on. Perhaps the difference is that a chair under a window would not draw the eye of a stranger looking around the basement for the first time, whereas a suitcase with broken glass on it jutting out of the wall underneath a broken window fits the narrative of a kidnapper escaping the scene. For me, the suitcase in the basement is a not-so-subtle message that the open window was meant to be seen as part of the escape route.

Chapter 11

A Bright Shining Lie.

Has it occurred to you that there are too many clues in this room?

Murder on the Orient Express, Directed by Sidney Lummet. 1974.

The Suitcase.

Someone moved the suitcase. John believed it should not have been under the window, although I don't know when he had last been in the basement, apart from all the times he had broken in. Patsy claimed to have not been in the basement that morning or the day before. But as both would later claim that some of the Christmas presents had been stored in the wine cellar, there was a good chance she had been down there on Christmas eve. What neither have confirmed was where the suitcase was originally stored before it was placed under the window. The reason for this might be that if it had been in a different room it would be difficult to explain why the suitcase was the escape ladder of choice rather than the red chair; and if it had always been in the games room it would be difficult to explain why John thought its placement under the window was so strange.

The suitcase belonged to Johns eldest son. Inside was a blanket and a children's book, which he conformed were his. The intruder theorists believe the suitcase was brought into the games room because the kidnap plan included putting JonBenét inside the case and taken away. It's possible that she could have fitted, but if she was taken from her bedroom and carried down with a blanket, why would you need a blanket? They may have seen the suitcase and believed it would be better, but remember, John and Patsy have never said the suitcase was in the games room. Looking at the small window and recess it would be difficult to get a suitcase out, so the initial idea doesn't even seem plausible. But then the intruder theorists say this was when the kidnapping turned into a sexual assault and murder. But that still doesn't explain why the suitcase is used to climb out of the window rather than the red chair or the white footstool nearby.

The Flashlight.
The black Maglite flashlight standing on the kitchen worktop was big enough to take three large batteries. John

and Patsy never claimed ownership of the flashlight, implying that if it was not theirs it must have been left by an intruder. That's not strictly true. What they said in every interview was that they were not sure if the flashlight was theirs, or they couldn't remember if they owned it or not. This leaves the door open for them in the future to remember at some point if its theirs, and that future point would be if forensic evidence linked them to it.

When it was first examined it did not have any trace of human contact. The flashlight, its adjustable head, and each of the three batteries were completely clean of fingerprints. I don't know if this means there are smudge marks from someone wearing gloves when they put the batteries on the flashlight, or there is nothing at all, meaning everything was wiped down with a cloth. But someone left it in a prominent position in the kitchen. When John, who has spent all morning walking around the house, is asked around 1pm to look for anything suspicious I am surprised that when he walked through the kitchen he didn't point to the flashlight.

If it had been left by the kidnapper, are we meant to believe someone has broken in with a kidnapping kit that included white cord, duct tape, stun gun, and a flashlight; they have gone up the stairs (in the dark), found JonBenét, perhaps gone back down and written the ransom note, then left the flashlight and gone back up to collect the child before carrying them down a spiral staircase in the dark and then to the basement, the darkest part of the house, without a flashlight? Or do they take her down to the basement, go up to write the ransom note, place each page carefully on the stairs then suddenly decide to kill the child instead, and in their rush to get down to the basement they forget the flashlight? I'm trying to think of any logical set of steps from the time of breaking into the home until leaving, which even includes killing JonBenét before writing the ransom note, but none of them makes any sense of how and why an intruder would about forget the flashlight, unless they were getting JonBenét some pineapple at the time.

Even the idea of more than one kidnapper remains problematic. One person takes JonBenét down into the basement and waits for their accomplice to write the note. The other person uses the flashlight to write the ransom note and places it on the spiral staircase. Do they then leave the flashlight and go down into the basement in the dark, realize that JonBenét is dead, and decide to make their escape? I am not saying the intruder leaving behind the flashlight is a lie, I just can't see a criminal leaving it on the kitchen table to find their way through a strange house in the dark.

But if it had been used by someone in the family that night, why leave the flashlight in open view for the police to see? It could have been put back in a drawer or hidden away in the garage. Why take all that trouble cleaning it? A few years after JonBenet's death a new theory came to light. The rounded end of the flashlight fitted the impact point of JonBenét's fractured skull. The flashlight becomes not only becomes something that an intruder would have, but now it's a possible murder weapon that someone in the family could use.

I disagree. If this was an item involved in JonBenét's demise, why not make it disappear along with the white cord and duct tape? You could argue that the metal flashlight would be the only item that could not be burned or flushed away like the others, but I still think it could have been hidden in the garage and no one would be any the wiser. So why was it left on the kitchen unit? Along with a dark top, black gloves, swag bag and mask, the flashlight is the epitome of a fictional burglar (or intruder). We have the blanket pulled away from the bed to show a child taken on the first floor, and the ransom notes on the spiral staircase. From here you can see the flashlight in the Butler's Pantry, go to it and from there you can see the basement door is open. You go down. In the games room is a suitcase under the broken window. The flashlight is another breadcrumb. Part of a trail of clues to lead you down a particular narrative path.

The Bowl of pineapple.

On the table in the breakfast room was a glass of iced tea that had Burke's fingerprints on it. Patsy and John (and presumably police officers and friends at the scene) stated Burke stayed in his bedroom until around 7am, then went downstairs and straight out of the house. We know Burke was awake from at least 6am and someone could have easily put something to eat and drink on a tray and taken it to his bedroom, but this never happened. Burke claims he just stayed in the bedroom because he didn't know what was happening. Next to the glass was a bowl of pineapple chunks and a large spoon. On the bowl you had Burke's fingerprints, and Patsy's.

This should not be surprising. It's their house. They have had most of Christmas day (up to around 5pm) for Burke to have a drink and something to eat during the day. But John, Patsy and Burke have all stated over the years that no one had anything to eat before they left for the party, and no one had anything to eat when they got back that night. Well, that's not strictly true. It's another case of people not giving a definite answer, not remembering, and not seeing anything that may be significant. Patsy would later state that SHE never gave JonBenét anything to eat. There is a reason for this. The bowl of pineapple was not brought up until a few weeks after JonBenét had died. By then everyone had locked into their story of coming home with JonBenét fast asleep and putting her straight to bed. There are a few variations on what time they got home, on who read to whom, whether john helped Burke make a toy while Patsy got ready for bed or John went straight to bed while Patsy packed for their trip. But the one constant is that JonBenét was asleep when they arrived home.

When the autopsy report confirmed that a piece of pineapple was in her stomach, and that it would have been eaten anywhere between two hours to thirty minutes before she died, the police remembered a photograph of the bowl on the breakfast table. And here we see a familiar pattern in the Ramseys narrative: it changes slightly every time the police make a new gain or come up with a new theory. As soon as they get the full autopsy report, John and Patsy push back the time they arrived home to try and distance themselves from when JonBenét died. If she could have eaten a piece of pineapple at 10.30pm, the Ramseys must claim they got home by 9 and were all asleep by 10.30pm.

The most obvious answer is that Patsy made Burke something to eat when they got home at 9pm. But this would also mean JonBenét was awake. The next answer is that at some point during Christmas day Patsy made Burke a bowl of pineapple and it had been left out overnight. But this would also mean JonBenét must have been awake when she got back and took a piece. You could have John and Patsy going to bed and Burke getting a bowl from the cupboard (which Patsy had put away and hence the fingerprints). In this scenario JonBenét could have woken up and come downstairs after seeing the lights on. Having a midnight snack with her brother, it would be easy enough for the conversation to turn to the presents they were getting when they got to Michigan, and the presents that were still in the basement.

All circumstantial, but all these things point away from an intruder being involved. A kidnapper does not break in and decide to feed their abductor while still in the house. If you start putting in the time JonBenét ate the pineapple, the time of the head injury and the time it took to write the ransom note, it means the kidnapper was in the house from possibly 10.30pm to 1am. So, the Ramseys simply never gave a direct answer to any questions about the bowl.

Perhaps the most telling item in all this was the oversized spoon. It's not something a parent would choose (although Christmas Day tends to be a time when children get what they want). Those who believe Burke had some involvement often outline a scenario where JonBenét comes down, takes a piece of pineapple, and in a moment of anger Burke hits her on the head with the flashlight. But if you are that angry you wouldn't need the next two pieces of evidence.

The knife.

Or, more precisely, a pocket Swiss Army knife. Found in the basement was Burke's Swiss Army knife. It had various blades and implements on both sides, and quite possibly could have left the two sets of small marks about three inches wide on JonBenét's body. It could have been used to whittle the end of the paintbrush. It could have also been used to cut the white cord. And there is another thing about the knife that we should mention.

When the housemaid Linda Hoffman was shown crime scene pictures by the police, she remembered that Burke had started to pick up pieces of wood that he could whittle into a sharp point and leave wood shavings all over the house. Eventually Linda took the knife off him just before Christmas. She placed it in a cupboard in the laundry area near JonBenét's bedroom. How it came to be in the basement on Christmas night is a mystery.

The Baseball Bat

To be more precise, two baseball bats. One grey, one black. Both metallic bats were found outside of the house. What is strange is that the black baseball bat had carpet fibres from the basement on it. When we talk about trace evidence such as DNA and fibres, there is a limit to how long they will last on moveable objects. If you leave an object outside it will also be subject to weathering. This is where wind, moisture, rain, and snow all affect how long evidence will last on that object. With the aluminium black bat, the only reason that carpet fibres would have been on it would be because it had only been outside for a short period of time. Strangely, the black baseball bat had no fingerprints on it.

With a neighbour who heard something metallic hitting concrete in the middle of the night, it has always been believed to be the weather grate, but it could have been the baseball bat. If the black baseball bat was in the basement at some point within twenty-four hours of it being seized, somebody must have put it outside, they must have also been wearing gloves or cleaned the handle. There is no clear evidence as to what cause the skull fracture, but I would suggest the end of the flashlight is about the same size as the baseball bat. Unfortunately, the bat is another piece of the jigsaw puzzle which no one seems to claim ownership. John said the grey baseball bat was Burke's but did not know anything about a black baseball bat.

The White Blanket and the Pink Barbie top.
The white blanket was believed to have been taken from the laundry area next to JonBenét's bedroom. The pink Barbie top was the item that she liked to sleep with in her bed with every night. Both ended up in the basement. The Ramsey's believed that the intruder must have taken them, but for what reason? The Barbie top was something JonBenét liked to sleep with. She might have been holding it when she was picked up, but the intruder did not need to take it into the wine cellar. The logical reason for taking the blanket would be to restrict JonBenét from struggling while you moved her out of the house, but a white blanket? Why not just grab her using the darker blanket that is already on the bed. The only thing I can think of is that although some areas of the basement had been carpeted, the wine cellar floor was concrete. There is no evidence that JonBenét was lying on the blanket when any sexual assault took place or when she urinated. This leaves us with the theory that even though she was dead, someone with a close connection to JonBenét may have subconsciously wanted to protect her from the cold hard ground. John said in interview JonBenét was wrapped up in a similar style to a papoose. At least this

piece of evidence, if it had been freshly laundered, would only contain forensic evidence from John and the person involved in JonBenét's death.

Chapter 12

When it's gone, its gone.

Two related but distinct emotional waves struck me. The first was that sense of horrified shame you feel when you know you're about to be caught in some act you will never be able to explain.

Stephen King, *The things they left behind*.

Although the body was found in the wine cellar, it has never been confirmed where in the house JonBenét died. There is a urine stain on the carpet in the boiler room next to the paint tray, indicating JonBenét was there at some point, and there is a piece of the paintbrush in the tray; but we still don't know the chronology of events. We can try working backwards. Somebody has wrapped her in the white blanket before putting her in the wine cellar. They must have had a reason why they did not put her arms inside the blanket. It may be because they wanted whoever to find her to see the cords around her wrists. We know that JonBenét was lying face down when she urinated. I don't know if there is any way of proving of the cord around her wrists were tied from the front. The cord around her neck was tied from the back, and shard of wood from the paintbrush were found in the boiler room outside the wine cellar door. So, it seems that at some point JonBenét was in the boiler room, and it also seems the garotte was made here. The head injury, the washing of the body, and the minor marks could have happened somewhere else.

The White Cord
It was used twice. One length was tied around the wrists, and another length used to form the garotte. I don't know if tests were done to see if they matched, as in they were both cut from the same length of cord, but they appear to be. We could also go further and ask how they were cut. A knife would serrate each piece of twine, whereas a pair of scissors would make a cleaner cut. Burke's Swiss Army Pocket Knife was found in the basement. This would no doubt not only have a selection of blades in it but could also contain a small pair of scissors.

The image of the loosely tied cord around the wrists remind me of those old black and white films of the damsel in distress lying on the train tracks as the locomotive gets ever closer. And like a movie, there is something not quite real about this set up. The cord was tied over the sleeves of

JonBenét's top, and even the coroner noted they were so loose the child could have easily slipped out of them. From that there is the implication the ties were put on when JonBenét was either unconscious or dead.

Some fibres from the white cord were found in JonBenét's bed. You could argue that someone has tied JonBenét in the bedroom to secure her wrists and stop her from struggling. The other option is that someone has cut the cord and then come from the basement to the bedroom. There is five inches of cord extending from the knot around one wrist. On the other wrist the cord extends over fifteen inches from the knot. This could have been used to bound the wrists together. We are also assuming the wrists were tied first (you don't need to tie her up after she has been strangled).

The question is, did the kidnapper bring a roll of white cord with them, or did they just happen to find some in the basement? I would argue that the kidnapper, as well as being lucky in finding a note pad and pen to write a ransom note, was also lucky to find a roll of white cord to tie his victim. It also means the kidnapper, clearly of high intelligence from the ransom note, seems to be making things up as they go along, and this now also includes changing motives. Which leads us to the next question.

When is a garotte not a garotte? A garotte is usually a short strip of wire or rope with handles on both ends. It is looped around the neck and can be tightened or released to control a person's breathing. The white cord tied twice around JonBenét's neck was not a garotte, but we will continue to use the phrase because it has been used so frequently in books, programmes, and podcasts. One of the most discussed things about this garotte was the intricate knot used to tie one end of the cord to the broken paintbrush.

A few years ago, I remember watching a programme about the assassination of President Kennedy, and a set was made where snipers had to shoot at a moving object from the same height and distance that Lee Oswald did in the school library deposit building. They also had to do it with the same rifle and within the same time frame. Some could not hit the target with three bullets, others could, but not in the time frame of 90 seconds. The presenter asked one old soldier if this was evidence that Oswald was not working alone that day. The grizzled marine looked up at the window frame and replied that there are times in life when you don't have to be a trained expert to hit the mark, you just have to be lucky. The black irony of his comment reminded me of the white knot.

Perhaps anyone could have tied the knot around the broken paintbrush. When people say only someone with experience of knots could have done it, they often bring in John Ramseys naval service, or Burke being a Boy Scout. What they fail to say is why the garotte needed such a large knot around the paintbrush in the first place. It makes no difference in being able to strangle JonBenét. You could have wrapped the cord around your hand. You could have used a simple knot to tie around the paintbrush. The knot is only to stop the paintbrush from slipping, but why? JonBenét could have been strangled by hand, but in so doing leave marks could indicate who had committed the crime. A cord tied twice around the neck gives no indication of the age or even gender of the offender. The length of cord from the back of the neck to the paintbrush was nearly twenty inches. The same length of the average adult's arm. It's a phycological distancing as well as a physical one, and it rules out a sexual motive. But in this intricate knot is hair from JonBenét. This could have only got there if the knot was tied around the paintbrush close to JonBenét's head and then pulled, and pulled, and pulled until the cord tightened slightly.

The only way the knot tied around the middle of the paintbrush makes sense is that it stopped the cord from slipping. It allowed the paintbrush to be held by two people, trying to be as far away as possible as they gently pulled, making both equally complicit, and equally innocent, of JonBenét's death.

The roll of cord could have then been disposed by various means. It could have been burned or flushed, or even thrown into a garbage bin. Which leads me to another question: where is all the wrapping paper and empty boxes from Christmas morning? Did the boiler room have a furnace, was there a fireplace, were the garbage men working on the morning of the 26th, and by the time police realised they were dealing with a murder the refuse had already been collected? In a landscape of discarded debris from Christmas day, who would miss pieces of white cord? But the white cord used as a garotte did reveal something. When the knot was finally unravelled forensic scientists found fibres from the clothes Patsy wore on Christmas night and the next morning.

The Artist's Paintbrush

The artist's paintbrush belonged to Patsy, who took up painting while she recovered from cancer. It had broken into three pieces, the middle used as the garotte, the brush end put back into the paint tray, the tip was never found. It would have been difficult for a young child to have snapped the paintbrush with their hands without breaking it in half. Although if you were to place the stick at an angle against the skirting and hit it with the base of your foot there is a chance it would break into three pieces. We know the paintbrush was broken in the boiler room because shards of wood were found near the paint tray. It's also believed that fragments of the paintbrush were found in JonBenét's vagina. As the paintbrush was varnished, this must mean it was either inserted into her when it was broken, or the tip had been stripped of varnish in some way. As the tip has never been found it could be that the kidnapper wanted a memento of their depraved crime, or it could somehow link the offence to an offender. But that reasoning could only apply to someone inside the house.

Duct Tape

The duct tape that had been placed over JonBenét's mouth was torn on both sides, meaning it had come from a roll that had been used prior to that night. Duct tape is notoriously difficult to break. I cannot see a young boy being able to tear it with his hands or teeth unless they made a cut into it first. It would also be difficult for an adult if they were wearing gloves. So, it is strange there are no fingerprints left by the offender unless they were very lucky, and John placed his fingers directly over where the kidnapper had placed theirs. From the lack of any signs of movement it is believed the tape was put over the mouth when JonBenét was unconscious or dead. Four fibres from the clothes Patsy was wearing Christmas night and the next day were found on the inside of the tape. The Ramsey Defence Team argued that those fibres could have come from being transferred from JonBenét's face when Patsy put her to bed. The fibres could not have come from the white blanket or the Barbie top. When police searched the house, they did not find a roll of duct tape.

At the start of the investigation police requested bank and phone records for the Ramseys but were refused by the D.A. because they were witnesses rather than suspects. They did manage to find that Patsy had gone to the local hardware store on two occasions in December. One till receipt showed she bought something that was the same price as a ball of white cord, and that it had come from the aisle that sold white cord. On another date she bought an item that cost the same price as a roll of duct tape, from the same aisle where duct tape was sold. Now, these aisles could sell a lot of items at the same price, so the most obvious thing would be to ask Patsy in interview if she had bought a roll or white cord and a roll of duct tape. Unfortunately, when interviewed a few months later she could not recall what she had bought on those two trips she made to the local hardware store in December.

Clothing

When JonBenét was found in the basement, she was wearing a used pair of boys long-johns, slightly too small for her, and a brand-new pair of size twelve underwear. I don't know if this refers to the age of twelve or an adult woman's size twelve. Either way, the underwear was far too large for the six-year-old. John said he laid his sleeping daughter on the bed and Patsy changed JonBenét into a pair of pyjama bottoms. There is no mention of changing underwear. Patsy was to state in interview a year later that JonBenét could have put them on herself before the party. But surely if you pull down the pants of a child asleep on a bed, any underwear that is literally twice as big as her usual ones will also come away? And if your child is asleep, why are you struggling to put on an old pair of boys long-johns?

The issue we have is that the accounts changed over time: from JonBenét going to bed in the red turtleneck (but who puts a turtleneck sweater top on a sleeping child?), to the underwear possibly being a present for JonBenét's stepsister, to Patsy (the wife of a multi-millionaire) later recalling she may have put a used pair of boys long-johns on her daughter that night, but can't remember. I don't know if the police found any used underwear in the JonBenét's bedroom. If JonBenét was asleep all this time, Patsy would no doubt have placed them into a laundry basket or next to the black pants JonBenét had worn to the party. But if they were strewn across the bedroom, doesnt this indicate that JonBenét was awake and moving around when she got home? And if they are not there, does that mean it is yet another piece of evidence that has gone missing? If Patsy claims that JonBenét must have worn the underwear to the party and that they were part of a set of seven that were meant to be a Christmas present, where did they come from? I don't know if an open packet of underwear was found in the basement along with the other presents, or it was part of the presents that were being taken to Michigan. Neither explains how they came to be on JonBenét. I also wonder if the used boys long-johns came from a bin bag of clothes next to the spiral staircase. One of the parties the Ramseys held before Christmas was for their local church. Is it possible Patsy was collecting clothes as part of a charity donation?

The brand new underwear was found to have traces of JonBenét's blood and an unknown piece of DNA, sparking a debate as to whether the DNA came from someone during the manufacturing and packing process. The long-johns also had the partial DNA of a male on them. But as these most likely once belonged to a boy this may not be the breakthrough in the case that some people would hope for. I don't know if the boys long-johns were once Burke's, or they were left by a school friend on a sleepover or bought back from camping. DNA can indicate gender but not age. If the urine had soaked through the underwear and the long-johns while JonBenét was lying face down, they would have drawn any DNA traces from one item of clothing to another when JonBenét was placed on her back in the wine cellar and the clothes began to dry.

Like most of the items found in the house, any forensic evidence on the clothes linked to the Ramsey's are complicated because it could have got there by an innocent explanation. Although, if fibres can be so easily transferred, such as those from Patsy's top found on the underside of the duct tape or inside the knot on the paintbrush, how come there is no DNA or fibres from the top John wore on Christmas night and the top he wore the next day on JonBenét's clothing? The only fibres that could be linked to John were black fibres believed to have come from the shirt John was wearing on Christmas night. These fibres were not on the white top, nor the used boys long-johns or the large new underwear, they were found on

JonBenét's skin near her genital area. This has been
disputed by the Ramsey Defence Team.

The Practice ransom note.
It is believed the writer of the ransom note tried a few
times, tearing out pages they did not use. Found in one of
the garbage bins inside the house was a page that had been
torn out of the notepad. It contained the line "Mr and Mrs
Γ". It was believed the downstroke at the end was going to
be the capital R for Ramsey, but for some reason the
kidnapper stopped. If it had ended it up being the ransom
note it would have been the first occasion that Patsy would
have been included. There are many theories about this
practice note. Some give plausible accounts as to why John
could have written the note, deciding to leave out his wife
in order to try and remove JonBenét from the house
without anyone else being involved. Others say Patsy
wrote the practice note, then realised it could lead to the
police asking her a lot of questions, so decided to focus all
the attention on John. It could also have been a kidnapper,
but I have no idea why he decided not to include Mrs
Ramsey in the final note.

For all three theories I wonder why the practice note
was thrown into a bin. A roll of duct tape has disappeared,

along with a ball of white cord, a piece of paintbrush, and possibly some clothing. So why not dispose of this piece of evidence as well? One option is that rather than the ransom note being one of the first things to happen in the series of events that night, it was in fact the last. After everything that had gone on, the writer of the note realised that it was almost dawn. The other items had been dumped in the night or dropped down a storm drain. The original part of the house was old, there could have even been a sewage pipe underneath or cesspit somewhere in the garden. But leaving the house now that people were getting up would ruin everything. So, the practice note was put in the bin and the final ransom note was written as the clock headed towards the time that John and Patsy had planned to wake up.

Chapter 13

Blood on the Tracks.

Marty Hart: Do you wonder ever if you're a bad man?

Rust Cohle: No. I don't wonder, Marty. World needs bad men. We keep the other bad men from the door.

True Detective, Season 1.

At some point in this book, I was going to refer to the James Stewart film, *Anatomy of a Murder.* It's the story of a court case involving a man who kills the man who raped his wife. In one scene the judge, defence and prosecution wonder how to use the word "Panties" without some people finding it amusing. The judge points out that there is nothing amusing about the circumstances in which a woman is raped and a man is killed. I have the same issue deciding what language to use when giving details about the death of a six-year-old girl. There are pictures and videos of JonBenét in which she is described as "provocative" and "alluring". The investigation includes a possible sexual assault. I cannot get change this as they are part of both the intruder theories and the Ramsey theories. But to write about some of the things that may have happened to this child makes me wonder what my moral duty is. Writing, reading, and watching true crime can be a therapeutic experience. The difficulty I have is how much information do I need to discuss to find the truth. My opinion is that there was no sexual assault in its legal definition, so I am not going to go into too much detail about certain things. You have the choice to read or go on the internet if you want more information. The last thing I should mention is that parts of the coroner's report is still restricted. This is still an ongoing investigation.

Blood.

Over two thousand exhibits have been seized since the 26th of December 1996, with over a thousand sent for forensic analysis. Although the house was seemingly clean, there were several items that contained JonBenét's blood. The first was the underwear she was found in. There are spots of dried blood, and spots of diluted blood where the body had been cleaned. The pathologists report mentions a one-centimetre abrasion in the hymenal orifice. I don't know if this scratch is where all the blood has come from. There is also blood on the long-johns, which appears to be linked to the same spots in the underwear.

Where things become more complex is that JonBenét's blood was also found on the white shirt that she was wearing. This may have come from the abrasions on her face and back, although they do not match up. There is also blood on the white blanket, but the spots of blood on the top and long-johns are so small that its difficult to see how JonBenét could have bled through her clothing and onto the blanket. And then we also have blood spots on the pink Barbie top. Four distinct spots on the front, although I don't know if they are spray spots, drops, or blood that has soaked onto the top from her skin.

Traces of blood were also found on the duct tape. JonBenét had been dead for at least twelve hours. The only way the blood could have got on the duct tape would be from the person getting traces of blood on themselves first, meaning the duct tape was put on JonBenét last. I don't know if any blood was also on the fibres from Patsy's clothes that were also on the duct tape. Traces of JonBenét's blood were also found on the cord used as the garotte. Again, I can't say if it was mixed with Patsy's clothing fibres. I think the most important factor in all this is perhaps the lack of blood found on JonBenét's body and the clothing. Could it be that there was a time when

JonBenét was wearing a different top, different underwear, and different pyjama bottoms, and they had visible blood stains on them. This would certainly have caused concerns if she had been found wearing those clothes, the most obvious would be the breaking down the kidnap motive straight away.

Urine.
The front of the underwear and long-johns were stained with urine. There was also urine on the carpet in the boiler room area, next to the paint tray, a set of golf clubs, and just a few feet away from the wine cellar door. The white blanket contains traces of urine. This could be from when it was wrapped around JonBenét, and she was placed in the wine cellar lying face up. It becomes more complicated when traces of urine are also found on the Barbie top. The top was not next to JonBenét's body when she was found. The only way forensic scientists would know to test for urine was because they could see it, we just don't know how and when it got onto the top.

Traces of urine were also found on the cord used as a garotte. This is strange if we picture her lying face down in the boiler room when the cord is put around her neck. It's possible the transference took place when someone has moved JonBenét, perhaps placing the cord onto wet clothing, or getting urine on their hands as they lifted her up. The only thing we don't know is if JonBenét's bladder emptied before or after she died.

Skull injury.

It is not known what caused the injury. When Burke is interviewed in 1997, he mentions that JonBenét could have been hit on the head with a hammer. Perhaps what he meant was a mallet, such as a ships' caulking mallet, often made of wood or rubber. If there was one in the house that night, chances are it would be either in the garage or in the basement. But this is all guesswork, to be added to the flashlight, golf club, and baseball bat and possibly causing the injury. It seems we could separate the object into two factions: smaller items that could be close at hand such as the flashlight, and larger items such as the baseball bat. This could make a difference as to the person holding it: a smaller person would certainly need to use a lot more force if they were holding a small object.

Maybe we should also try to picture is the position of the person with the object and the position of JonBenét to get the type of injury she had. If she was lying on the floor, someone would have to stand near her head and swing an object as if using a golf club. If JonBenét was on her hands and knees and a baseball bat was swung as she crawled forward, the damage would be the same. The other option is that someone taller than JonBenét has stood over her and brought the object down onto her skull. And did the blow come from someone standing to her right, as the fracture is on the right side of the skull, or did it come from someone standing in front or behind her. This changes things slightly, as a blow from the side tends to imply that JonBenét was standing still at the time. A blow coming from someone in front or behind JonBenét could be that she was running away or towards the other person.

Some people believe that JonBenét could have been put into the suitcase, lifted to the basement window, and then dropped, causing the skull injury. But again, pathologists believe this injury happened anytime up to two hours before she died. This has been questioned due to the lack of blood and bruising around the brain. And it has also been answered by surgeons who explained that the brain controls every major organ in the body, including the heart. A serious head injury would have slowed the heartbeat down to such an extent that it would have also affected the flow of blood. The injury would also affect the lungs, causing some people with similar injuries to use a ventilator to stay alive. Even minor pressure on the neck for someone whose breathing is extremely shallow would result in death. And if JonBenét did go into a state of complete unconsciousness being dropped in the suitcase, how did she get the other injuries?

Neck Injury.

The strangulation is another piece of the jigsaw that does not fit what this crime was initially seen to be. Strangulation itself is quite an emotive method of hurting someone, usually a jealous partner or a person very close to the victim. We could also say that on most occasions both parties are facing each other. An adult can sometimes gain sexual pleasure from being strangled, and one person can gain sexual pleasure from strangling another person. But what about the injuries to JonBenét's neck that were not caused by the cord?

The autopsy report mentions previous injuries to her neck, some superficial, others powerful enough to cause bruising. These must have happened during the hours from when she was home to when she died. The bruises on the front of her neck could be from someone trying to hold JonBenét in place while using the other hand to change JonBenét's clothes or wash her down. They would also leave visible red marks. Taking JonBenét to hospital for the head injury would have raised concerns of child abuse as soon as those marks around the neck were seen. But if a ligature was put around the neck, and the ligature was believed to be the cause of death, those previous marks might be missed.

And if it was an intruder and they were wearing gloves, why would they need a garotte to strangle JonBenét? The garotte cord is so long I can't see how it would be used as part of the offender's sexual pleasure. They could have easily controlled JonBenet's breathing by using one hand. And even if we ignore the fact that experts have said the head injury happened at least thirty minutes before she died and say that the strangulation and skull fracture occurred almost at the same time, what order are we talking about? Does this intruder stop strangling JonBenét to look for an item, come back, and then hit her on the head? And why? If you are determined to kill someone then strangulation is more effective than a skull fracture. You could also argue why any intruder would cause the other marks found on JonBenét's body.

Marks on face and back.
There are two sets of marks which have gained a level of importance over the years. They consist of two puncture wounds on the side of the face, and two similar puncture wounds on the back. Again, if no witnesses at the party mentioned them, they must have happened when she got

home. The pathologist at the time made no mention of them being electrical burn marks. For those who side with the intruder theory, the belief is that they were caused by a stun gun. But this doesn't fit the motive to the method. Why try and incapacitate a six-year-old child you can easily tie up, put tape over the mouth, and carry away from her bedroom without a struggle? If it was a taser used twice in the basement I am still not sure as to the kidnappers reasoning. Surely, it's not part of a sexual fantasy, or are we saying she was still fully conscious and fighting back hard enough that the suspect had to stun her?

Another theory is that the case that the two sets of marks are so similar they must have been caused by the same object, such as the prongs from a piece of model train track. As there is a model train set belonging to Burke in the basement this seems to be more plausible, but surely the police collected all the track pieces from the house, and if need be, test all of them for any signs of JonBenét's DNA.

We are still left with the question of why JonBenét has these marks. I cannot think of any reason why an intruder could cause them. I don't know if the suitcase under the window had belt buckle type straps inside, and the marks have come from the metal prongs. This leaves us with someone in the house causing these marks. John or Patsy could have made them, but if it was anyone then surely it would be Burke? It could have been part of a game that got too violent. It could have been after the head injury, and she was prodded twice hard enough to puncture the skin to see if she was still alive. What I would like to know is if the two puncture marks on her back had gone through the white top she was wearing when she was found, and if there were two blood spots around the collar. Or do they match the four blood spots found on the Barbie top?

When do these injuries happen in our timeline of events? It looks as if there were six occasions when some sort of violent act has taken place: the abrasions on face and back, abrasion in vagina, marks on neck, skull fracture, garotte, duct tape placed over mouth. None of these make sense if she was asleep when an intruder enters the bedroom. Nor do they make any sense if the intruder causes the injuries while they are in the basement. On a final note, to me the marks do not appear to be as alike as everyone suggests. Its hard to see the second abrasion on the face. I always thought the marks looked more like those caused by hobby scissors than anything else. There was a pair in the basement.

Chapter 14

Silent Witness.

Was it doubted that those who corrupt their own bodies
conceal themselves?
And if those who defile the living are as bad as they who
defile the dead?
And if the body does not do fully as much as the soul?
And if the body were not the soul, what is the soul?

    Walt Whitman, I Sing the Body Electric

Stomach

A portion of fresh pineapple was found partly digested in
JonBenet's stomach, meaning she was alive at least sixty
minutes before being strangled. Logically, if the skull
fracture was enough to put JonBenét into a coma, then she
must have eaten before this. If so, we can narrow down the
skull injury happening to within an hour before she died.
But first we should clear up the issue of whether the item in
her stomach pineapple or something else. Some say that it
was mucus, or fruit she had eaten at the party. I will go

with the pathologist who saw it and said it was a piece of pineapple.

The interesting thing seems to be that the Ramseys cannot explain the bowl of pineapple in their Breakfast Room. In those first accounts both John and Patsy say they put the sleeping JonBenét straight to bed, in one account even reading to her while she was asleep. This was originally bordering into 10.30pm territory, when we are only ninety minutes away from her death; but in later interviews the Ramseys say they were home before 9pm, and all asleep by 10.30. Perhaps John and Patsy may not have known about JonBenét eating pineapple when they gave their first accounts on that first day, or they believed it wouldn't be found in her stomach. But when they saw the full autopsy report a few months later they knew that changing such an important part of the scenario of carrying the sleeping child straight to bed would make some people think that the parents had lied.

And if John and Patsy have lied about JonBenét being asleep as they arrived home that night and putting her straight into bed, we must ask why? One answer is that she was awake when they got home, and she never made it into her bed. On the first point, her being awake might mean the police would ask Burke questions about what happened when they got home. Every minute she is awake is another minute closer to her death, and another minute that John, Patsy, and Burke must account for. The further away they are from midnight, the more chance that an intruder has come in while they were asleep.

And what if the story of JonBenét being asleep is correct? John claims he read a story to JonBenét and then went down and helped Burke with a model before putting him to bed. It is unlikely that parents would let a six or a nine-year-old stay up when they are about to go to bed, but perhaps it is possible to say goodnight to someone who is almost ten, and then go up to your bedroom on the floor above not realizing that a ten year old might want to stay up and play on a brand new game console. He could have woken her up and asked JonBenét if she wanted to play a computer game, and even offered to bribe her with some pineapple. It sounds more plausible than a kidnapper taking her out of the bedroom and while writing the ransom note giving her a piece of pineapple from the bowl.

Although we could argue that if anyone in the family were involved, and knew JonBenét had eaten a piece of pineapple, why didn't they put away the bowl? Why wipe all fingerprints off a flashlight and leave the bowl? Could it be that the breakfast room does not link to any other room apart from the kitchen. You cannot see it from the spiral staircase, and don't need to go through it to get to the basement. The only thing of note is that directly underneath the breakfast room window is the weather grate, and the broken basement window.

Lower Body.

From the autopsy report -

Bladder: The bladder is contracted and contains no urine.
Genitalia: The upper portions of the vaginal vault contain
no abnormalities. The prepubescent uterus measures 3 x 1
x 0.8cm and is unremarkable. The cervical contains no
abnormalities. Both fallopian tubes and ovaries are
prepubescent and unremarkable by gross examination.

To me, the idea of an intruder having a sexual motive doesn't make sense. If you are there to make money from a kidnap you want to get the victim as quickly as you can and then be as far away from the scene as possible. If you are there to commit a sexual offence, you might bring with you the same items (tape and cord), but you wouldn't waste time writing out the ransom note. So why does this theory exist that she had been sexually assaulted in any way? It is one of the few ideas that links both those in the intruder theory camp, and those who believe at least one of the Ramseys were involved. You have an intruder who starts off kidnapping JonBenét, even going so far as to leave a ransom note, then change their mind and sexually assault her. Another theory includes Burke playing a game with his sister and things go wrong (including the vaginal injury being self-inflicted). You have John Ramsey sexually assaulting his daughter, and JonBenét threatens to tell someone. Patsy cleaning/assaulting JonBenét as a form of corporal punishment for wetting the bed. The Ramsey theories, and the red marks/washing of this area, seems more probable than the idea of a stranger committing a sexual assault and then cleaning down the body to get rid of any DNA, if only because there is no reason to get her dressed afterwards.

The pathologist's report includes: *"On the anterior aspect of the perineum, along the edges of closure of the labia majora, is a small amount of dried blood. A similar small amount of dried and semifluid blood is present on the skin of the fourchette and in the vestibule."* There is also: *"A 1 cm red-purple area of abrasion is located on the right posterolateral area of the 1×1 cm hymenal orifice."* Finally: *"A minimal amount of semiliquid thin watery red fluid is present in the vaginal vault."*

It seems that something was inserted, small enough not to rupture, but it did cause a 1cm cut. It is possible that it was the tip of the paintbrush; but why would someone take the time to intimately clean JonBenét when there is no evidence that their DNA would be found there? Could it be that the tip of the paintbrush had been altered in some way, such as sharpened, and this is what has caused the abrasion. Perhaps the reason for cleaning JonBenét is not to get rid of forensic evidence, it is to clean out any wooden splinters which could be linked to the paintbrush. But this only makes sense if the altering of the paintbrush could be linked to a specific person. We may never know the answer, as the tip of the paintbrush has never been found.

With regards to forensic evidence, if someone had taken the time (taking the clothes off, getting a cloth, washing down JonBenét, putting the cloth back, getting JonBenét dressed, with the clock always ticking) to remove any possible forensic evidence from JonBenét's body, why didn't they also take the oversized underwear and long-johns with them to make sure they had left nothing behind. It's not as if they were part of any fantasy of how the intruder wanted JonBenét to be found. They had wrapped her up in a white cloth before they left.

DNA.

There are over thirty trillion cells in the human body, making each person unique. So how do you tell the difference in the DNA between a six-year-old girl and a grown man? For a start even in a small sample there will be

X and Y chromosomes which will tell you if the person was male or female (sorry millennials). You will also be able to tell the persons basic genetic make-up, such as Asian, white, or black (sorry O. J. Simpson). With more information we might be able to say if they had been born with any medical conditions. With a full match of the genetic pattern or sequential numbers you will be able to say that DNA left at a scene can be matched to a person. But now we come down to the same issue we have today that we had in 1996, the first is that DNA from a crime scene can only be matched to DNA from a particular person...If you have the DNA from that particular person. This can be from a database or taking a DNA sample. In 1996 you needed quite a bit of DNA to be able to identify certain genetic markers. Add to this the way DNA was collected at the time and you can see why the O. J. Simpson defence team put so much effort into disputing the audit trail of blood found at the scene rather than who the blood might belong to.

The next issue is that DNA can also be a moveable object. Contact with an item of clothing, which is then picked up by someone else and taken home, means your DNA is now inside a house that you have never physically been in. Another example would be the pink Barbie nightgown found next to JonBenét in the wine cellar. As well as having four spots of blood and traces of urine, it also had three spots containing Burke's DNA, and one spot containing both Burke and Patsy's DNA on it. A reasonable expectation as they all live together.

But we are not finished. The techniques in how DNA samples were tested have also come under scrutiny. In 1996 every time you made a DNA test you used up a piece of the DNA, and the item the DNA was taken from. Take a cutting from the long johns to test and chances are you will destroy that piece of fabric. The situation isn't too bad if it's blood or semen that is visible as you usually only need a tiny fragment to get a result. But even here we get into problems with cross contamination. In 1996 an item that was going to be tested for DNA might not have been kept in a sterile environment. And it still comes back to being able to match the sample with a suspect.

With JonBenét there are three points where relevant DNA has been found: The fingernails. These were cut with clippers during the autopsy. From a fingernail on the right hand, a male and a female's DNA was found, but both were too weak to be able to make any comparisons. On a left fingernail was also DNA from a male, but again the sample was not good enough to be able to compare it with anyone else. But before we move on, there is a serious flaw with these exhibits. Every fingernail was cut with the same clipper. What this means is there could have been different DNA on different fingernails, and they have now mixed. It is also believed the clippers may have been used on other people without being properly sterilised. Another important aspect is that although the results show a mixed partial profile, which could mean more than one person, they also show that the DNA did not come from skin cells, which means JonBenét did not scratch anyone.

Male DNA was found on the Long-Johns. These would be the same well-worn boys long-johns that Patsy was never sure for the first couple of years (until the DNA showed an unknown profile) if she put them on the sleeping JonBenét on Christmas night. The last test showed that there could be at least six different profiles on the long-johns. None of them were good enough to be able to check one a database. One of these profiles, even though only partial, did match DNA found on the underwear. It was found in a spot of blood. Again, there is another issue with this DNA result. Imagine of every letter and character on this page is your DNA, and the blank space around them is your item of clothing. Over the next full stop a drop of JonBenet's blood lands on top of it **O** When someone sees that drop of blood, they test it for DNA because they know it is going to come back with a result. It turns out to be JonBenét's blood. Underneath is your full stop, your DNA, because this blank page is your item of clothing and your DNA will everywhere. But there does not appear to be anymore checks on the long-johns. Instead, the DNA report merely states that on the point where JonBenét's blood was found in the underwear there is also an unknown male profile that matches the long-johns. Another blood spot was tested, and the result was another male DNA, but this was even too weak to compare against the other DNA found. To me, this looks as if the used long-johns had been through the wash before being put on JonBenét.

A spot of blood on the garotte that belonged to JonBenét was checked and came back with DNA. This was not believed to be the same DNA found on the long-johns and underwear, which means there could have been more than one intruder, or the DNA was not good enough to be able to check against anything else. A spot of blood on the cord around JonBenét's wrists was also tested. Again, there was a male profile on it, not the same as those found on the long-johns and the underwear, but not good enough to be able to match with any individual at this point.

There is simply not enough DNA cells available to confirm that an intruder was involved. The DNA has either been corrupted by other elements, such as contact with other chemicals, different DNA merging with the original cells, or there was simply not enough of the cells to be able to get a profile due to the contact being extremely limited. This is often described as "Touch DNA", or "Trace DNA". These are tiny fragments of skin cells that we can leave anywhere, and they can be taken anywhere. All samples taken from the wine cellar probably fall into this category.

Starting with the DNA under the fingernails, how does this link to an intruder? We know JonBenét did not scratch them. She may have pressed her hand into the intruders clothing and trace DNA was transferred by those means, but wouldn't she have been wrapped in the white blanket when carried down into the basement? With the long-johns, trace DNA was found in the area stained with urine. But again, isn't our kidnapper wearing gloves, and if it been transferred from their clothing, wouldn't it be more likely to find trace DNA on the back of the long-johns and white top when she was picked up off her bed and carried two floors down into the basement? Although trace DNA could have dropped from the intruder's face when they were watching over JonBenét. That does not answer how trace DNA was found in the underwear.

An intruder who has left no fingerprints anywhere in the house, including the bedroom and the flashlight, who has left no measurable DNA such as in the bedroom or around the basement window, somehow leaves trace DNA on the brand-new underwear. How? If there was a sexual assault, wouldn't the underwear have been taken off. If this was happening while she was being strangled, wouldn't the intruder still be wearing gloves? These are all questions regarding the flaws in the intruder theory, but because we are talking about evidence tests in 1997, we cannot rule out the intruder theory altogether. A forensic examination in 1997 compared to an examination today is rather like comparing the Wright brothers first take off to the invention of the jet engine. Not just in technology, but in the mindset of those at the crime scene. This also raises a far more interesting question: If we were to treat all the evidence today with a far greater understanding of DNA, does this mean everyone who has ever been ruled out of the investigation because their DNA didn't match be put back onto the suspect list? And should the Ramseys also be put back onto that same list?

The Ramseys can keep demanding DNA checks. If any new DNA testing comes back to them, they have the defence of living in the house. The most recent results show a total of six different DNA profiles found on various items and JonBenét herself. These are all partial matches and mixed profiles, including those of an unknown female. I doubt if anyone is saying that six people entered the house that night; and it also shows that even with advances in technology it doesn't mean this case will be solved by DNA alone.

But we should also mention Joseph James DeAngelo. He was dubbed *The Golden State Killer*, who committed at least thirteen murders and over fifty rapes between 1974 and 1986. He had left semen at numerous crime scenes, but it was only in 2001 that police started matching all the DNA into a national database and realized just how prolific DeAngelo had been. Unfortunately, the police had only started taking DNA from those charged with an offence long after DeAngelo had stopped committing them. It was not until 2017 when DNA testing had improved to the point that genetic markers could be used to look for familial DNA that detectives were given another chance of finding the killer. They could use the full profiles of DNA left at crime scene in the 1970's and 80's to see which cells were linked to the persons ancestors. Using what is often called "Familial DNA", the police found about twenty people in the database who shared common characteristics with DeAngelo's great, great, great grandparents. These could be cousins, aunts, nephews, who had been arrested for various offences. From this standpoint detectives narrowed down the list of suspects until there was only one. After checking the DNA he had left on a tissue in his garbage can, DeAngelo was finally arrested for murder in

2018, over thirty years after he had last broken into someone's home.

Chapter 15

Have you heard about the Midnight Rambler?

There are two possible solutions to this crime.

Agatha Christie, *Murder on the Orient Express*.

At 5.52am on the 26th of December the police were told there had been a kidnapping. When they arrived both parents were fully dressed. The ransom note was bizarre, but that didn't mean it wasn't real. They were told the house alarm had not been turned on that night. The doors and windows on the ground floor had been checked and were all closed, but there were possibly six spare house keys in existence. Have I mentioned the dog yet?

The Ramseys had a dog. A small white Bichon called Jacques. Or to be more precise, they had two small white Bichon's called Jacques. Patsy had bought the puppy for the children; but when it became ill Patsy had the dog put down, and rather than tell the children, she simply went out, got the same dog and gave it the same name. When

Patsy and JonBenét started to travel across America to compete in beauty pageants and John was busy at work, they would give the dog to their neighbours the Fernie's to look after. On Christmas Day John took the dog over to a neighbour's as they were going to the party later and then they would be leaving early the next morning. It is a remarkable stroke of luck the dog was not in the house that night.

When police arrived the next morning both John and Patsy named a few people they believed could have taken their daughter. As such, rather than focusing on the house, the police diverted resources into looking at a possible terrorist group, disgruntled employees from Access graphics, one of the hundreds of guests who had attended the house in the last month, and people who had worked in the home. Add to this, someone who may have seen an article a few days before Christmas on John Ramsey being the director of a billion-dollar company, or someone who may have seen JonBenét at one of her child beauty pageants, or who had seen JonBenét when she performed at the local mall and then appeared in the Christmas parade.

It would be wrong to say that the police could not find the body of a six-year-old girl that morning. They were looking for an escape route, not a grave. They had also been told to treat the Ramseys with respect. The Ramseys were rich. And to be fair, this was a kidnapping for money, so why wouldn't police think a child was being kept by someone somewhere else until the financial transaction had taken place. That morning the list of possible suspects seemed to be growing on an hourly basis.

For all the accusations against the police, the most famous being from John, who would often claim that he told detectives "By all means look at us, but just don't stop there. Unfortunately, they did"; or that "the police believed they had their suspects on the 26th of December and didn't bother investigating anyone else", this is simply not true. The police made many mistakes at the start of the investigation but treating the Ramseys as the only viable suspects was not one of them. The police went on to speak to over seven hundred people who were treated as possible suspects, and even today the list is still growing.

Once the body was found there were more suspects added to the list. Sex offenders, serial killers, people who had committed the crime of breaking and entering, information from members of the public about people they suspected might have done it. In some ways, the Ramseys had shown America that no child was safe from a stranger attack. Boulder was a nice white town with a strong sense of community. A strange individual walking the streets would have stood out like a sore thumb, unless they looked just like everybody else, and they managed to get into a house without being seen.

Any suspect that climbed in through the basement that window that night needed three things to be in the frame: the Means to commit the crime, a Motive to carry it out, and the Opportunity to do it. The means. Did they have the capability of getting to the address without being seen, do what they did, and also get back to their own home. Were they physically capable of carrying out a kidnap and then later a murder? We can't rule out the intruder being female, but they must have been physically capable, so, lets put the age range between twenty and sixty. If they wrote the ransom note, they are also highly literate.

Motive. Was there an incentive, such as money, revenge, or even an overriding sexual fantasy, which enabled them to make the fateful decision to enter the house? The main motive the moment they entered the house had to be money, otherwise there is no logical reason to write the ransom note. It is extremely rare for something so apparently carefully planned to take such a drastic turn and become a possible assault and then a murder. We know there are people who do break into homes with the intent to steal and commit sexual offences, but again, they don't write ransom notes. The caveat to this is that JonBenét knew the person involved.

And what about opportunity? Here is the strangest aspect of this case. I would rule out anyone living further than a twenty-mile radius from the house, if only because there must have been an element of preparation involved. By that I mean not only the use of cord and duct tape, but someone also who must have had known of the family and a basic knowledge of the layout of the house. No one is just walking around that night checking windows and doors and just happens to see the broken window in the basement and decides to break in to kill a child. And having knowledge of the house includes knowing it well enough to walk around in the dark. Time is also a factor. The night before they would have alerted the dog, the night after and no one would be home.

So, we are looking for someone physically capable of breaking into a large house, but unable to carry out a child. Someone who can write out a detailed set of ransom demands, and then cashes in nothing. Someone who has all the chances to get away with one crime, and then decides to stay in the basement and commit a totally different one. Whichever way we look at this we seem to end up with more than one type of intruder. It leaves us again with the ransom note. We have someone that is well educated and knows quite a bit about John's business and personal matters. But John was upper management. His business associates were probably all in their fifties and would have spent more time on the golf course than in each other's back gardens. If their aim was to hurt John, they would have done it in the boardroom, not the basement.

There is the possibility of it being someone who knew the Ramseys by way of being in their home through work such as repairs, gardening, catering. They could have overheard about John getting a bonus of 118k. They could also have known about the broken window in the basement, and where JonBenét's bedroom was. But the chances of a blue-collar worker being able to be such a threateningly eloquent wordsmith does not match the image of a man who works with his hands. But that morning both John and Patsy were able to span the social spectrum of suspects and come up a few names. We shall start with the one they both mention.

Linda Hoffman.

Linda gave birth to her first child before she was 18 and had spent most of her working life doing low level domestic jobs. Now in her late forties, she been a housemaid for the Ramseys for nearly two years. Her husband had done some general maintenance work around the house (using duct tape and cord?). Her two adult children and at least one of their partners had all been in the house just a few weeks ago to help get the house ready for the parties. They had even been down in the basement to get the Christmas trees from the wine cellar.

When the Ramseys told police about Linda they mentioned that she was desperate for money. What they failed to mention was that they had already agreed to loan her two thousand dollars for car repairs, and that she would pay it back from her salary. Patsy told police that Linda had also said to her something about JonBenét being so pretty, and if she (Patsy) was ever worried about her being kidnapped. This may have been a strange thing to say, but perhaps Linda had recently seen the film playing in cinemas, *Ransom*, in which a millionaire businessman has his child kidnapped.

Linda would know every loose floorboard and creaking door and could have easily moved through that house in the darkness. She could have taken the notepad and pen any time before Christmas, bringing them back with her on the night. She could have woken the sleeping JonBenét before taking her downstairs, and JonBenét could have silently complied. But I find it difficult to believe Linda would have the brains or the inclination to carry out this crime. When the police spoke to Linda on the 26th of December, she said she had been at home on Christmas night with her husband, which leads us to another interesting aspect of the intruder theory. There could have been more than one person involved.

Linda may not have broken into the house that night, but she might have known who did. She could have given that person the ransom note and told them where to go in the house. If her fingerprints were found on the ransom note she could say she had probably picked up the pad while cleaning. But how does a kidnap plan end in murder? The simplest answer is that JonBenét recognised the person trying to take her. Trapped in a house with a child who might be able to identify you doesn't leave you much choice. Even if you continued with the original plan and got the money, you would still get caught eventually. Linda's husband, Mervyn, was a blue-collar worker in his fifties who liked a drink. I doubt if either could write the ransom note. Linda's children could have been involved, but now we are getting into "Faction" territory, where no doubt every individual in the group would want a sufficient amount from the multi-millionaire father.

Another scenario could involve someone who wasn't personally linked to Linda Hoffman. She could have hired a mercenary who was willing to do it. But now it feels like we are entering movie territory. I doubt if you can just walk into a bar and ask if there is anyone willing to kidnap the child of amulet-millionaire; and if you could, I doubt if you would start the price at just 60k each. No matter how we look at Linda Hoffman as a suspect, there are some serious flaws. She clearly could not have written the ransom note even with the help of a dictionary let alone copies of Patsy's handwriting. If it had been someone she had hired, this well-educated professional criminal would have demanded much more money for their share. As for a family connection, I think there is something else that someone in Linda's position may have considered first. If she had any criminal propensity or links to any criminal organisation, there was a far easier way of getting some cash. A housekeeper with a key who knew the family were going away could have arranged for the home to be burgled. They wouldn't even have to smash a window to make it look like a break in. It had already been done for them by John.

Business Associate.

That morning John mentioned a few people. These were former employers who had left for various reasons, but John believed they might have had a personal issue with him. Rather than look at any individual, we shall deal with the whole company. I believe there were about six hundred employees at the time, with about two hundred based in

Boulder. Although we should not rule out the possibility of someone travelling a long distance to commit this crime, we now reach a serious block in the road. We can all agree that someone had to know this house. They had to know the outside, if any neighbours could see or hear anything that might give them away. They had to know how to get in, which means getting close enough to the house to be able to look through the windows, and the weather grate. They had to know the inside well enough to know John and Patsy slept on the top floor. I think we can rule out the office junior who spent all day at the photocopying machine, or the lady in accounts who worked part time and had three cats. In fact, we can rule out a lot of staff. Chances are they had never had a conversation with John, and very few of them would know the house well enough to be able to get around in the middle of the night.

But desperate people do desperate things. Theoretically any member of staff could have broken in, so we must rule them out by other factors. There is distance, there is the personal issue of them having family or being missed at any point during the night, and there is the physical aspect of the crime. John may have been able to climb in through that basement window, but how many others could? America Psycho may have been a fictional account of a murdering businessman, but it's doubtful if anyone in

John's work would be willing to risk being convicted of killing a child for the sake of being let go. The ransom note is also telling.

When Det. Arndt asked John, Fleet White, and John Fernie if they could give any information on the ransom note, both Fleet White and John Fernie gave their views, but John remained silent. With the writer of the note respecting his business, I am surprised that John did not mention the ransom demand was the same as his Christmas bonus. I also think that if it was someone from John's company the last thing, they would want to do is draw attention to themselves by asking for the same amount as their bosses Christmas bonus. But at no point during those three pages did John say that the writing looks like, or the phrasing sounds like, an ex-employee.

Chapter 16

Narrow Margin.

I constantly remind people that crime isn't solved by technology; it's solved by people.

Patricia Cornwell.

Out of the hundreds of suspects the police investigated, a few stood out more than others.

Bill McReynolds.

With long white hair and beard, the former university lecturer had become the town Santa, with some of the children believing he was the real thing. Bill McReynolds had played Father Christmas at the Ramsey house for the last three years. It's not surprising. He was also old, slightly overweight, and wore glasses. He became a suspect because of the seemingly strange links between him and the death of JonBenét. The first is that his own daughter had been abducted at Christmas when she was a child twenty years before. She was taken into a basement and forced to watch as another child was sexually assaulted.

Even more bizarrely his wife then wrote a stage play about the whole thing, with a major plot change in that one of the children was murdered.

I don't know if the Ramsey's were ever asked if they knew about this before JonBenét had died. If they did, it means that on Christmas night they had one story of a child being abducted and killed, and a housekeeper having asked them if they were concerned about their own daughter being kidnapped. But Bill was not our man. The chances of him being able to climb through a small basement window would be nigh on impossible. The police still questioned him though. They stopped when he told them he had major heart surgery just a few months before Christmas and struggled to use the stairs. What is more interesting is that Bill became a media suspect. The idea of Santa Claus killing a child on Christmas night garnered a lot of news coverage.

Michael Helgoth.
Michael Helgoth was a local idiot. He worked in a junkyard and was into weapons. He allegedly told a co-worker before Christmas that he and a partner were going to come into money, about 60k each (half of the ransom demand). It is also alleged that he once said he wondered

what it would be like to crack a human skull. After Christmas he was very depressed. On February 14th, 1997, the day after the District Attorney gave a speech about the list of suspects narrowing and soon there would only be one name left, Michael committed suicide. This was after recently separating from his girlfriend. A former partner would later say that she believed he had an inappropriate interest in her young daughter. He also wore Hi-Tech boots, the same make found in the wine cellar. He may have even had a baseball cap with the initial SBTC on it (allegedly). He could have known people who had worked for John.

His suicide was later doubted due to the fact the right-handed Helgoth had shot himself in the left side of his stomach, using a pillow to deaden the noise. Why would a man reach over to fire a bullet into himself that may not have even been fatal, and why use something to silence the gunshot when you lived in the middle of nowhere? Helgoth also brings in another new feature about the case. In his room was a stun gun. If Helgoth did have dark fantasies about children, using the scenario of two people entering the home, it is possible that someone stayed up in the kitchen writing the ransom note while Helgoth was with JonBenét in the basement. By the time the writer had got back down into the basement she was already dead. It certainly explains why there was such a drastic change from one motive to another. But again, the writer of the ransom note is clearly well educated. If I was going to partner up to commit the crime of the century, it wouldn't be for sixty thousand dollars, and it wouldn't be with someone who liked to go around in double-Demin and a mullet. And even if I considered myself a master criminal I just can't see Michael being clever enough to not leave a single piece of evidence in the bedroom or the basement. Neither his boots or his DNA matched the crime scene.

John Mark Karr.

What if the motive had always been sexual and the ransom note was a ruse? John Mark Karr is a waste of space who was into kids. A few years after the murder he started chatting to someone online about accidentally killing JonBenét during a sexual act. He was eventually tracked to the Philippines

(Victory?), where he was awaiting trial for child sex offences. Detectives from America brought him back for questioning. Within minutes it was clear he didn't do it. He was miles away from Boulder on 25th/26th December. I'm not going to say much more about him because he doesn't deserve the air of publicity.

Chris Woolf.

Chris Wolf was an out of work journalist who tried to sue the Ramseys after they named him as a possible suspect in their book, *"The death of Innocence"* (its full title is, *The death of Innocence: The untold story of JonBenét's murder and how its exploitation compromised the pursuit of truth.*) The book was published in the year 2000. In it the Ramseys point out that Wolf lived in Boulder (like Patsy) had similar handwriting to whoever wrote the ransom note (like Patsy), he had a degree in journalism (like Patsy), and he knew someone who worked for Access Graphics (like Patsy). An ex-girlfriend reported that he could not remember if she saw him on Christmas night, that he seemed to be following the case too closely, and he kept hinting about writing an article that the Ramseys were involved in some way in their daughter's death. I don't know why the Ramseys believed Woolf was any more of a viable suspect than any of the others, nor do I know why Mr Woolf would want to take this through the civil courts, as the initial costs would be extremely expensive, and if he lost, he would be liable for further costs. But then the only way he could lose would be if he was guilty.

Fleet White

Their old friend Fleet White was also eventually named by the Ramseys as a suspect. The man who had invited them over to spend Christmas at his home, and possibly the last nonfamily member to see JonBenét alive, was also one of the first people on the scene that day. So how did he end up on the list? Things seem to change about a week later at JonBenét's funeral. Fleet and John were seen to get into a very heated conversation about John and Patsy not yet being interviewed by the police. They may have been grieving parents, but speaking to police while their memories were still fresh would have helped catch the person who killed their daughter. The relationship became more tense when John and Patsy went on national television the next day to give their accounts. This was while Fleet was being spoken to by police again about why he didn't see the body when he opened the wine cellar door. It is not known what Fleet White said in his interviews.

After this, John's legal and publicity team put forward the idea that Fleet knew about Johns business life, Fleet knew about John's personal life, Fleet knew the house, Fleet was the one who made the silent phone call to the police on the 23rd, Fleet had turned up that morning and supposedly looked into the wine cellar without seeing anything, had touched the suitcase, and Fleet even went back down to the wine cellar after the body had been recovered.

Fleet White was to eventually give eighteen voluntary interviews to the police: that's nine hundred percent more times than John. In the first interview (which took place within days of JonBenét being found) he told police that the Ramseys left his home on Christmas night around 9.30pm. Perhaps this is also what caused the rift. He was also adamant he saw and smelled nothing in the wine cellar that morning. Perhaps the most obvious reason why Fleet is innocent is that on Christmas night at no point did Fleet wish John and Patsy a Merry Christmas, and then take them aside to say that if there was any major incident or tragedy to give him a call in the morning. He was at the scene because Patsy wanted him there. He was a significant witness because John took him down into the basement and the wine cellar. He was a suspect only because the Ramseys said so.

Gary Oliva.
The last person is someone considered to be almost a total stranger. Any preparation for this crime was minimal. They took a chance when they saw the open window in the

basement. They found a pad and pen and wrote the ransom note. They took JonBenét down to the basement and killed her because they had mental health issues. It was a few years later that registered sex offender Gary Olivia was arrested for possession of drugs. Inside his rucksack was a photo of JonBenét and a stun gun. It transpired he was living just a block away at the time of the murder. He was even photographed at the vigil outside the house a day after the murder was announced. Someone also came forward a few years later and told the press that on the day JonBenét was found, Gary had called him to say he had hurt a child.

The problem with Gary and all these suspects comes down to the same three things: Means, Motive, Opportunity. If this was not a random act, how come the last part wasn't completed? Kidnappers don't usually kill the kid and leave them in the house to be found. Sex offenders wouldn't want to waste time writing a ransom note. The clock is ticking, and with every second there is the fear of being caught. Some theorists start with the idea that when the intruder climbed in through the basement window, they were doing it for money, but they cannot say why the price is so low. They then claim that the motive is one of revenge; they were going to make John suffer before his daughter's body was found. So why not string it out for days or even weeks, or why not stage the body into the most horrific scene they could think of? The intruder theorists then say there was a sexual motive. So why bother getting her dressed afterwards? No one motive seems to match all the probable course of events, and this leads us to the next issue.

If you believe in the intruder theory, then you must believe the ransom note is real. In that case we cannot get away with the fact that it could take up to thirty minutes to write. The intruder theorists answer is that someone broke in that evening while the Ramseys were at the Christmas party and had a couple of hours to spare. This is clearly rubbish. How do you account for the practice note found in a bin downstairs. Are we saying the intruder cleared everything away, but didn't feel the need to get rid of this particular piece of evidence. What if the Ramseys had come home and found it? If this was a jigsaw puzzle it would feel as though some of the pieces fit some of the small details, but the bigger picture doesn't quite match.

It's just as difficult if you try to move events around: You take the girl to the basement first, tie her with the cord and stick duct tape over her mouth. You go back up and spend thirty minutes writing the note. Then you go down to the basement and get turned on enough to forget about the money. Or did the intruder carry out a sexual assault and choking as part of some fantasy role play and then went up and wrote the note as a way of making John suffer? We still have the fractured skull to contend with. Did the intruder use the flashlight, clean it, and then leave the murder weapon behind? Did they use a baseball bat, clean it, and then leave it where it would easily be found?

And it still does not explain how someone breaks into the home with the duct tape, cord and possible stun gun they brought with them, then kill a girl and leave her wrapped in a blanket they took from a cupboard near her bedroom. And in-between give her a piece of pineapple, inflict minor injuries, carry out a sexual assault, and cause a skull injury. Do any of our intruders fit every single piece of these scenarios no matter which was we put them? No.

Gary Olivia had mental health issues. That is not to say anyone suffering from schizophrenia is a danger to others. It is far more likely they are a danger to themselves. He could have watched JonBenét, followed her back to the house, and when the family left for the party that night, he came in through the basement window (although the whole idea of this broken window simply blowing in the breeze seems to be taken for granted), and decided to come back that night. But I think Gary Oliva can be ruled out quickly and easily by answering just one simple question: Gary, spell "attaché" for me.

As for Fleet White, his motive would not have been money, so can we really see him going through this whole charade of a fake kidnapping? For those who think that John Ramsey was involved, they dismiss his notion that he could not have done it as he was a good family man with no previous convictions. Shouldn't we also extend that courtesy to his employees and all the other suspects of a similar standing?

Chris Wolf was a writer. He may have disliked John Ramsey for getting rich from a business that would eventually kill the printing press. He may have disliked Patsy's southern way of doing things. He may have even disliked the police and District Attorney to the point of goading them to get him treated as a suspect just to seek fame; but it's all circumstantial. We still don't have enough. It's the same with Michael Helgoth. He wore Hi-Tech boots, but so did hundreds of other people in Colorado. He had neither the wit nor the capacity to be a criminal mastermind. The same is true of Linda Hoffman. The money worries, the mention of kidnap before the event, knowledge of the Ramseys business and personal details, all lead us to her. But she was one of the few early suspects that the police ruled out after a thorough investigation. She was interviewed on numerous occasions and her home was searched. We know that there was a similar notepad and pen found in her home. But would a cleaner and her stumblebum husband be able to write so well? Would they be able to get a professional criminal to help carry out the kidnap; and if they did, would any criminal of that calibre risk carry out a job for such a paltry sum? If Linda Hoffman had been involved in the original kidnap plan and later found out it was murder, I am pretty sure the District Attorney would have made a plea bargain deal for her to name the killer.

So, who was our intruder? As well as being of above average intelligence, they were also supremely lucky. They were not being seen by any of the neighbours both before and after the event. The family dog was left with a neighbour that night. The alarm system was not turned on. Johns' adult children were not staying at the house. There was no lock on the weather grate. The broken window was not locked or linked to the alarm system. They managed not to cut themselves as they reached in to open the window. The basement door wasn't locked or alarmed. John and Patsy said they were sound asleep by 10.30pm. JonBenét was not sleeping in her brother's room that night. There was a note pad and pen on a desk drawer. You had the piece of duct tape, the white cord, a large black flashlight, and possibly a stun gun, and none of them had the intruder's DNA on them. In fact, there are no unknown fibres left by this unknown stranger. That's quite an impressive record for someone who started with one motive and ended with another. Let's not forget that for those who say the police messed up the crime scene by letting people walk all over the house, JonBenét's bedroom was sealed that morning, and only three people went into the basement before her body was found. And so, if you believe that an intruder's DNA was found under a six-year-old child's fingernails, an old pair of soggy boys long-johns, and the underwear Patsy cannot recall JonBenét wearing that night, how did they manage to leave no trace anywhere else. As such, the moving DNA, found on movable objects, does not prove someone broke into the house that night.

Chapter 17

Burke.

I don't care how close you are: in the end, your friends are gonna let you down. Family. They're the only ones you can depend on.

Tony Soprano, The Sopranos. TV series.

If it was not an intruder, then it was someone in the house. Applying the same rules, there must be a Means, Motive, and Opportunity for any theories relating to anyone in the family. The biggest advantage that John, Patsy, and Burke have is that of opportunity. There is nearly eight hours from getting home to the police arriving to be able to present the scene that greeted the police at 6am that morning. At the start the focus of suspicion was always on John and Patsy, but this changed later to include their son Burke, who at the time of JonBenét's death was just a few weeks away from his tenth birthday. It is important to remember the age of ten is when a person is deemed as being criminally responsible in a court of law; in that they know the difference between right and wrong and must accept the consequences of their words and actions. It has its flaws, such as not considering any mental health or social situations which may have stunted a child's intellectual and emotional growth; but let's not pretend children are not capable of doing bad things.

If we go back to 1993 in Liverpool, England, and the abduction, torture and killing of Jamie Bulger by two ten-year-old boys, we can see there are always going to be people whose blood is wired differently even from a very young age. Parents and grandparents will take great delight in telling stories of how their now adult offspring did something memorable as a child like hit their sister with a golf club, and these stories can be rolled out at every social gathering to embarrass the younger generation, but does that make them a killer? Readers of true crime will often find that some people are marked from a young age because they are considered outsiders or shyer than their peers. This does not mean children within the autistic spectrum or have a physical defect are inherently bad. What we can say it that most people are shaped by their first few years. How early childhood affects everyone can be vastly different than someone going through the same events. Before Burke was nine, he had lost one half-sister to a car crash, and his mother was diagnosed with Stage 4 cancer, often a terminal condition. How that shaped his view on life and death is difficult to say, but it must have had an impact.

Like many boys in 1996, what Burke wanted for Christmas more than anything was a Nintendo 64 console. At the time there was a call to ban certain video games because they were too violent. To be honest, the graphics in 1996 were not that good. The law would eventually legislate some games as only suitable to be sold to those over the age of 18. How anyone could enforce what boys did in their own home was never disclosed. It didn't matter. It transpired that what was more damaging to a child's mental health was the amount of time, especially young boys, spent playing these games. Rather than play outside or read a book, hours would be wasted in front of a screen where actions did not have consequences and acts of violence would be rewarded. Links would later be made in relation to substance addiction and people suffering similar effects of withdrawal systems if they were not allowed to continue playing. But is any of this a possible reason for Burke to be involved in his sister's death?

Early Christmas morning. It's dark. Burke wakes up first. He wakes up his younger sister. They go upstairs to their parents' bedroom to wish them a happy Christmas. They wait for a more suitable time and then all go downstairs to open Christmas presents. The parents like the capture the moments. After a few pictures of Patsy, JonBenét, and Burke opening presents, Patsy goes into the kitchen to make them a big breakfast of pancakes. Pretty much a lot of people's experience of Christmas day.

But let's go back a bit. There is John's account of going over to a neighbour's house on Christmas eve to collect the new bike for JonBenét, but it's quite possible all the other presents had been stored in the basement, especially the wine cellar with its wooden latch on the top of the door to stop children from finding them. Let's go back a bit more. If there is one thing that most nine-year-old boys want before Christmas day, it's a flashlight. The idea of Santa coming into the home and bringing presents might have still been believed by JonBenét, but Burke had probably used that good Boy Scout sense of his to have a look around the house. Having grown taller in the last year, a wooden latch might not have been a problem, especially with a chair or a younger sister on his shoulders.

I am still not sure what presents everyone else opened on Christmas morning. Patsy got a bike. I don't know where this had been stored. There is one account that Burke also received a bike. I believe Patsy had ordered one for him, but it was meant to be for his birthday a few weeks later. If so, where was this kept? We know that JonBenét got a gold bracelet with her name and the date of *12/25/1996* on it. This I find a bit strange as its usually peoples date of birth that is more important. JonBenét also got a life-size doll which looked like her. Patsy had sent off photographs and some of JonBenét's clothes to have the doll specially made. I don't know what else Burke got apart from the Nintendo and a few games. I also don't know if the computer console was set up in the living room or Burke's bedroom.

Later that day a few children from the neighbourhood come over. I think the relevancy of this is that it shows a level of sociability within the family. For all the rumours about the parents, I think this was the sort of house where other kids were happy to go to, perhaps even down into the basement. It's also in the forensic window where fibres and DNA from others could get onto JonBenét (and under her fingernails) and still be there when she was eventually found. That afternoon JonBenét rides her bike around the garden. I am not sure if Burke goes out with her. John comes back from the airport. Later, they go inside to get changed for the party, and John takes their dog over to a neighbour's house.

At this point there is a story of JonBenét refusing to wear the same clothes as Patsy, black trouser pants, and a red turtleneck sweater. Patsy sticks to the same outfit, while

JonBenét wears a long white sleeve top with a star on it. Patsy does not say if JonBenét is wearing the underwear that is twice the size of the ones she normally wears. This is strange because we know JonBenét had three elastic ties in her hair. If anyone had put them in place, and no doubt brushed her hair, it would have been Patsy. More importantly, we have no idea of what Burke is doing all this time, or if he wants to go to the party.

They all go to Fleet White's house five minutes away. Other children are there. Again, we are in the forensic window where DNA can be transferred. They play games. Depending on which account you want to believe, the Ramseys leave anytime between 8.30 – 10pm. Burke stays in the back of the car as Patsy make two visits to drop off presents. I have never seen any statements or reports that JonBenét went out of the car with Patsy to help deliver the presents or how long Patsy spent chatting. They arrive home.

In Burke's first account (without his parents present), he claimed that after parking the car in the garage they all walked into the hallway, with (the awake) JonBenét and Patsy walking slowly up the spiral staircase while he and his father helped fix a model (train?). Burke was aware they were going to take a plane early in the morning. Within thirty minutes he goes to bed, with Burke recalling that he may have heard voices in the night, but that it may have also been a dream. I should add that although this differs from John and Patsy's accounts, Burke does not mention anything about eating pineapple.

In the morning Burke recalls being woken up by Patsy calling for John, not JonBenét. We can say that its before 6am, when Burke was expecting to get up and get ready to go on a plane. Patsy comes into Burke's bedroom, stands in the doorway, looks around, and closes the door. Burke can see his mother is upset and knows their flight is within the hour, yet he never feels the need to get up and find out what's happening. After that John, just in his boxer shorts, goes down the spiral staircase and reads the ransom note while Patsy calls the police. There are around five minutes before the police arrive in which John presumably goes back upstairs to get dressed and then back downstairs to check the windows and doors on the ground floor. Burke never mentions that he ever hears his father calling for JonBenét. In all interviews Burke claims that he stays in his bedroom.

I don't know if officer French rings the doorbell or the Ramseys are waiting for him with the door open, but there must have been some sort of information passed in the hallway, which is just below Burkes bedroom. Officer French is taken to see the ransom note on the floor near the spiral staircase (Patsy has been with it for five minutes and not picked it up and read it?). He goes up the spiral staircase and looks into JonBenét's bedroom. It would be strange if neither John nor Patsy were with him, asking questions, demanding answers. On the same floor, Burke is still in bed. Officer French then opens Burke's door, looks around Burke's room with a flashlight, and goes out again. In all interviews Burke says even though he knew it was a police officer he stayed in his room because he thought his father was in trouble. You would think every boy would have gone to find out what was happening. I suggest that someone must have told Burke to stay in his room, but no one has ever admitted to saying it.

Other people start to arrive. Again, Burke would have recognised the voices of the White's and the Stine's, and we must also assume Patsy was extremely emotional at this point. But for some reason he stays in his room. It's not until about 7am that Burke finally comes out of his bedroom, escorted by John, and goes down to the front door to a waiting car ready to go to Fleet White's house. Does Patsy say anything to him, does he take anything with him such as toys or a change of clothes? Nobody seems to know. Burke leaves the house that morning never to return. Whatever he left inside that house would forever be a memory.

Does any of this prove Burke was involved in the death of his sister? The most common theory in relation to Burke is his link to the bowl of pineapple on the breakfast table. Burke's fingerprints are on the bowl. There is a large, oversized spoon with it, not the sort of thing an adult would give to a child. In the crime scene photographs the bowl of pineapple appears to be unfinished. There is also a glass of iced tea next to the bowl with Burke's fingerprints on it as well. The bowl was never considered important until the autopsy showed that JonBenét had eaten a piece of pineapple within an hour before she died. By then John and Patsy had locked themselves into the story of JonBenét being asleep when they got back home and being carried up to bed. Burke was not spoken to again until a couple of weeks later. This was by a child psychologist rather than the police. When shown a photograph of the bowl of pineapple he seems to avoid answering any questions about it.

The theory is that Burke was eating the bowl of pineapple on Christmas night when the parents are asleep. JonBenét comes down and takes a piece. Burke has struck her, possibly with the flashlight, knocking her unconscious. This puts John and Patsy out of the picture at the start of events, and so nobody calls for medical assistance. Now we have a ten-year-old boy knowing he has done something wrong, but not knowing how to deal with the situation.

When we go back to the James Bulger case in England and the two ten-year-old boys walked the two-year-old Bulger out of the shopping mall and onto a piece of waste land. They threw stones and a tin of paint at him, they assaulted him (including a sexual assault) and fractured his skull, causing him to become unconscious. Being so young they were simply not sure if he was dead or not. To cover up what they had done they then placed the boy on the train tracks in the hope it would be seen as a terrible accident. A pathologist later reported that Bulger had died before the train hit him, but some of his minor injuries had been caused after death. With JonBenét Ramsey it's possible that the marks to her neck and back were by being prodded to see if she if she too would wake up.

But let's get rid of being hit by the flashlight and instead have JonBenet go down to the basement of her own free will. Burke tells her there are more presents in the wine cellar. Father Christmas does not exist. The presents are partially revealed. JonBenét is told not to say anything and is stopped from leaving by being grabbed by the neck. A baseball bat later found by police outside near the butler's pantry door had fibres on it consistent with fibres from the carpet in the basement. We have the pineapple in her stomach, marks to her neck, an injury consistent with being hit by a baseball bat, and then Burke tries to wake her by jabbing hard into her skin. It kind of fits, but what about the marks on her genital area? Although most sexual offences on children are committed by males, we also must include the idea that JonBenét herself has placed something inside her and started to bleed, causing the start of events. But let's say that so far everything that has happened to JonBenét could have been done by Burke. The final act is where it gets difficult for me to believe he was involved.

Burke was a Boy Scout. One of the things he could have learned was basic knots. But even if he left marks around JonBenét's neck and had accidentally knocked her unconscious, I don't believe he would try to cover these acts up by creating a garotte and strangling her. Why would he even think that using a piece of broken paintbrush would make any difference to the garotte? Why would he even think of washing her down and then putting on a change of clothes would deflect attention away from himself? There is also something else which leads me away from Burke being solely involved. I don't know if he was tall enough to reach the latch which was on the top corner of the wine cellar door. But even if he could reach it, after leaving the body in the wine cellar wrapped in the white blanket, would the next thing on his mind be to twist the latch back and lock the door? It's possible, but would he then think to put a suitcase under a broken window. And we still have the last literary part of the puzzle to contemplate. Surely no one believes that a nine-year-old boy wrote the ransom note. For all I know Burke may have been a child prodigy, a junior Moriarty of crime; but I doubt if even he would think to hide his own style by pretending to write like his mother.

I suppose the idea that the nine-year-old Burke did it helps us resolve this mystery and almost clear our own conscience. We have a child under the age of criminal responsibility. We have the scenario of this starting off as a tragic accident over a piece of food. We have parents protecting their only living child for his tragic mistake and facing the rest of their lives being accused by an unforgiving public. For us, trying to make sense of a senseless death, it is the result that we almost wish was right. Justice is served, and the quality of mercy allows us to be gentle. But that doesn't mean it's true. Part of it still comes down to not knowing the sequence of events, and the fact there could be over an hour between the start of things happening and JonBenét's final moments. A child may have rushed to cover their tracks in relation to hiding a crime, but an adult would have taken their all night to lead police towards a different one.

Chapter 18

John.

Kathy, I'm lost, I said, though I knew she was sleeping.

I'm empty and aching and I don't know why.

    Paul Simon, *America*.

When it comes to fiction and true crime we like to think
there is always a moment when the suspect gives
themselves away. A gesture or word. Sometimes we miss it,
other times we catch a glimpse of what appears to be a
minor detail, and it is only later we realise its significance.
For John it seems to be the moment he finds his daughter.
There is duct tape over her mouth. How tightly its stuck we
don't know, but John pulls it away. He tries to remove the
ties around her wrists, then removes the blanket and picks
her up, presumably under the knees and armpits. But
before he can carry her up the stairs he must turn her in an
upright position because the body is so stiff her arms and
legs do not bend. No doubt her neck was visible and the
white cord of the carotte was hanging down in front of him.
The smell of death within the urine-soaked clothes must

have also been noticeable. John comes out of the wine cellar, through the boiler room, into the hallway, and goes up the narrow basement stairs all with his arms outstretched and holding his daughter by the waist because her body is too rigid to be carried by any other means.

As he comes out of the basement door, he places the lifeless stiff body down onto the rug near the front door. Detective Linda Arndt comes over and leans down to look at the deathly white face of JonBenét. It is at this point John looks at Arndt and asks, "Is she alive?" For all the emotional storm raging around him, this phrase seems contrived. She has been dead for at least twelve hours. It must have been obvious. But I don't blame any father for hoping that his daughter is still alive. Even a fool's hope is better than nothing. So, is there another moment that blurs the intruder theory and brings John's involvement into sharper focus?

When it comes to the window in the basement, is John telling the truth about him breaking it a few months before Christmas? I can understand why John may have chosen the basement window rather than one on the ground floor. It was late at night, Patsy and the kids were away, and he wasn't going to wait for a locksmith or a glazier. What I can't understand is why John didn't get it fixed afterwards. It's a small square piece of glass in a wooden frame. A general handyman could have done it within an hour. We know they had a gardener. We know the housemaid Linda Hoffman and her husband often did small repair work. But apparently, Patsy cleared up the glass when she got back. Are we saying that the window in the children's games room was never opened again until Christmas night, causing a large piece of glass to fall on the floor, and a small piece of glass to land on the suitcase? There is also another issue. In an early interview Burke says that he was there when John broke the window. In a later account John explains this by saying that he went through that basement window a few times. Surely this means he also had it repaired a few times as well, or did he go through that window a few times in the last few months? John also claims to take off his suit before he went down into the narrow weather grate and through the window in the summer. What difference does this make? Well, such a thing might explain if any of John's arms or leg hair was found at the scene the day after Christmas.

Perhaps the strangest thing is not John breaking the window a few months before Christmas, but the window itself. In his book, *The death of Innocence*, John Ramsey states that the basement windows would often blow open during a storm. Looking at the photographs and crime scene video, the three windows are all flush with the interior wall, and the latches appear to be of the type more often found on internal cupboards. It would not have been difficult for a grown man to have put his weight on the wooden frame itself and push the window open, certainly easier than smashing a window.

It is also strange that the middle window was broken, as John would have to use his left hand to turn the latch. It would have made more sense when standing outside to have broken the end window to your right, allowing you to use your right hand. Its only standing inside the basement itself that the middle window seems the obvious choice, as you can open the latch with your right hand. There is also the issue of the recess being extremely narrow, possibly less than two feet wide. How did John, nearly six foot tall, manage to crouch down and kick the window. Its possible he did it by sitting on the grass, but it seems more possible that the windowpane was broken another way, possibly by someone else.

Looking at the crime scene photographs you can see large sharp pieces of glass still inside the window frame. I don't know if anyone tried to put their arm through it after JonBenét's death to see if they could reach the latch, but if you had kicked it with your shoe, it would have fairly easy to continue kicking until most of the glass has gone. John has already done the hard work by completely lifting off the weather grate to sit on the grass and kick the window. A few more taps would have cleared any sharp edges.

We should ask why John never said anything to the police that day. Again, it's not a question of lying to the police, it's about saying nothing and leaving a trail of clues for the police to come up with the intruder narrative by themselves. When he finally mentioned it over fourteen hours after initially calling the police, John said he didn't think that the open broken window was strange that morning because he had done it in the summer, it was the suitcase underneath it he wanted to mention. This was the same morning his daughter had been kidnapped. Perhaps it's not so much what people say and do that eventually gives themselves away, it's their silence and lack of action that reveals the truth.

John seems to have been linked to his daughter's death by way of a sexual motive. It is claimed he was abusing JonBenét that night and somehow, either she threatened to tell, or the abuse became more violent, she ended up dead. John is also linked to the garotte by way of the knot on the paintbrush because he was in the navy. He also finds the body, planning to do so with a witness to essentially create the illusion of shock. We have a possible means, motive, and opportunity. I just don't know if John would have wrapped JonBenét in a blanket or included her favourite barbie top to be placed next to her. It's quite possible he could have caused all the injuries to JonBenét, but why? If he needed to kill her, he didn't have to fracture her skull, he didn't have to cause the marks to her face and back, and he didn't have to tie the piece of paintbrush to the garotte. He was ruled out of writing the ransom note. Although there are parts of it that read like a business letter and uses words more familiar in the corporate world; I think a man in his position would have made it shorter.

John, like everyone else who lived in the house, can be forensically linked to the body. Perhaps what is more interesting is the lack of evidence. His fingerprints are not on the ransom notes, nor are they on the flashlight, the pineapple bowl, around the broken window frame, or the suitcase. He took the duct tape off JonBenét's mouth, but I have never seen any record of his prints being on it, nor do I know if his DNA was found on it..

John had carried JonBenét into the bedroom and placed her on the bed, so his DNA and clothing fibres from what he was wearing on Christmas night will be on her top. When he went into the wine cellar the next morning his DNA and fibres from his new clothes should be there. He loosened the ties around her wrists, so his DNA could be on that; although I don't know if he ever tried to loosen the cord around her neck or touched the broken paintbrush. He carried the body upstairs, more transference. He placed her on a rug, then after she was moved again, and he gave her one last hug goodbye. All of this makes it difficult for John to be accused of any crime through forensics. And in his defence, did he do anything wrong?

When police arrived, John seemed to be very reserved. Again, who knows how anyone would act if they believed their daughter had been kidnapped. But John didn't spend time comforting his wife, nor did he start asking the police questions about what they were going to do. Strange, as he had already disregarded the kidnappers first demand of not calling the police. If you were a former Navy personnel and now a millionaire businessman, you would want the FBI to be landing by helicopter on the front lawn if necessary. You wouldn't want to be waiting for the kidnappers to be in control. You would be calling some very influential people in Government to help find your daughter.

That morning John and Patsy both had ideas as to who might be involved, with John naming former work colleagues. We are still in the time span where everyone thinks it's a kidnap and are waiting for the phone call; but I feel that what is missing is a sense of urgency. If you suspected someone of taking your daughter and give the police names, at what point would you have expected the police to kick in those doors? Perhaps John has been informed that the FBI are on their way and so is waiting to speak to them. We know that John looked around the basement that morning, although the time he did this changed during later interviews. From 8am he is confined to being near the telephone in his office. This must be like the waiting room in a hospital where no one knows what to say and do. When 10am comes and goes, we are still waiting. Officers make note that John doesn't ask any questions.

Around 10.30am forensic officers have finished and some of the detectives go back to the station for a briefing with the FBI. John still has not mentioned the suitcase and open window in the basement. But nor has he mentioned the link of 118k and his Christmas bonus, nor the fact that he had spent time in the navy at a small foreign harbour in the Philippines which had the initials S.B.T.C, and that its bank notes were printed with the word "Victory". Perhaps he doesn't say much as he is nowhere to be found.

By 12pm Detective Arndt was concerned enough about John's disappearance that she called headquarters and asked for extra help, but police chiefs were still in a meeting with the FBI. John comes back but does not say where he's been. It would be interesting to know if Arndt mentioned to John that the FBI were finally on their way, something that could change the dynamics of the investigation and what would happen to those in the house. Arndt does note that John's demeanour seems to have changed dramatically. At around 1pm Arndt called the station again. She is told by an FBI agent to keep John "busy" until they arrive. This means give him something to do but keep an eye on him. There is the contentious issue of the phrase, "Search the house from top to bottom" to look for anything out of place. Taken at face value, most people would start in the top rooms. For John to not mention to Det. Arndt anything about the basement window and the suitcase at this point is strange.

We are now in the basement. John does not go straight through the boiler room and open the wine cellar door. Instead, he goes into the games room, a room he has already searched, and mentions the open window and suitcase to Fleet. Why tell Fleet, it's not his house, he's not a detective. Now they come out. Rather than turn left and go to the other storeroom which is closer and appears not to have been searched by anyone, they go back towards the stairs then turn towards the boiler room. The wine cellar has no connection to JonBenét whatsoever. There is nothing in there which would help John with the kidnapping of his daughter. I don't know if Fleet told him he had looked in the wine cellar earlier but did not see anything because there was no light. John twists the latch and opens the door. He calls out almost before he turns the light on. It could be that the hallway light is on, and he sees the white blanket and realises there is a body in it. But then what exactly was he looking for when this was still a kidnapping investigation?

The FBI and more detectives finally arrived at the house around 1.20pm. Things kick into gear. There is a discussion about moving everyone to a local hotel to talk to them individually. While this was happening, a detective heard John talking on the phone about getting a private plane to Atlanta as soon as possible. He tells police that he has an urgent business meeting to attend. The strange thing about this is that he should still be waiting for the kidnappers to call. Also, He had a private plane booked to go to Michigan to stay with family for a few days and then fly back to go on a cruise. At what point did the idea of having a meeting come up? He refuses to stay in a hotel. This is another strange decision. If you believe a small foreign faction has killed your daughter, a hotel, possibly with the police on guard, would seem the safest option.

The family leave in the afternoon to stay with a friend. And here is another issue. I must wonder how a man who has spent all morning waiting for a kidnapper to call, then all afternoon dealing with the suspicious death of his child, managed to get a lawyer for him and Patsy within two hours of leaving the home? John would later say that a lawyer friend spoke to him that day and said they had a friend in law enforcement (D. A's office?) who didn't like what they saw in relation to the Ramsey's being suspects and asked to represent him. How does a conversation with a man who had just found his murdered daughter get round to needing legal advice? These are wealthy white Christians, probably the least likely group in America to be framed by police. At 9.30pm when detectives come by to see how they are doing, John is waiting with his brother, who just happened to be a lawyer. There is also a doctor present (who is also a lawyer). John tells police Patsy is too distraught to speak (confirmed by the doctor/lawyer), and he cannot leave because he is looking after her (confirmed by his brother/lawyer). John promises to give the police an interview as soon as they are ready. Just as police go to leave, John finally tells them about the broken window and the suitcase.

Some people say that those involved in family murders will do anything not to find the body, and so the fact that John did proves he wasn't involved. I would suggest there are two issues with this. The first is that if he knew the FBI were coming (to deal with a kidnap) they could have cleared the house and taken everyone away to be interviewed apart from him, as he had to be there if the kidnappers called. This would have meant there would have been no witnesses to finding the body. The FBI, believing that John and the police had searched every room, might have not conducted their own search. And as John could never implicate himself by asking if anyone had done a search, JonBenét could have been left in the wine cellar for another twenty-four hours. Arndts request for John to look around to see if anything was missing was John's last chance of having a witness for when he found the body. There is also another reason, John may not have been involved in her death, but that doesn't mean the rest of the family are innocent.

Chapter 19

Patsy.

Well, I've been afraid of changing cos I
Built my life around you,
But time makes you bolder, children get older,
I'm getting older too,

    Stevie Nicks, *Changes*.

The investigation begins with Patsy. It's her voice that starts most documentaries and podcasts as she phones the police. Quite often the Image that follows is from their first television interview just a week after JonBenét had died. In it she appears drugged. Little wonder as she had just buried her only daughter. But we need to go back. Christmas day. It's early. Burke wakes up JonBenét, they go and wake up their parents, and then all go down to open their Christmas presents. Patsy, so often focused on presentation, wears just her dressing gown and no make-up as she and her daughter smile at the camera. There are one or two photos of JonBenét and her new bike. The next morning when police arrive and ask for a recent picture of JonBenét, they are told the video camera had a low battery and was put on charge yesterday. No mention of any photos taken. Fleet White tells police he has pictures from the party, and these are the ones taken to be developed that morning. It's not until the evening that police seize the Ramsey's film camera.

After opening presents Patsy cooks a breakfast of pancakes. The children play with their toys while John drops off the dog to a neighbour then takes more presents to the airport. It seems that on one of the busiest days of the year Patsy is going to be left to do everything. Some of the neighbourhood children come over and play. There is no mention of anyone having lunch. When John comes back, he takes JonBenét outside to ride her bike. It possible that Patsy has been trying to finish packing, although like many mothers she probably spent a lot of time on the phone wishing family and friends a Merry Christmas. That afternoon there is an argument between Patsy and JonBenét over wearing identical outfits, with Patsy giving in and allowing JonBenét to wear a white top rather than the red turtleneck sweater. They leave around 5pm for the five-minute drive to the White's.

There doesn't appear to be anything out of the ordinary at the party. Other children were also there. They leave between 7.30 and 9.30pm, depending on which interview you listen to. They stopped off at two other houses for Patsy to wish them a Merry Christmas. I don't know if any of these people saw JonBenét. Patsy stated that on Christmas night JonBenét fell asleep in the car. The time they arrived home varies from 10pm -10.30pm in the first accounts, down to possibly 8pm when Patsy is interviewed a few months later.

John carries the sleeping JonBenét from the car in the garage, up the spiral staircase and into her bedroom with Patsy following behind (presumably Burke stays downstairs for the next couple of minutes). There is no mention of taking JonBenét to the bathroom, even though she regularly wet the bed. There is also no mention of how the waistcoat JonBenét was wearing that night came off, or why Patsy didn't think about putting a diaper on JonBenét. In later interviews, Patsy says she leaves JonBenét wearing the white top but takes off her black pants and puts on a pair of pyjama bottoms. She doesn't mention anything about putting any underwear on JonBenét, but this could mean she has left on the ones JonBenét had been wearing for the party. She also does not specifically say if the pyjama bottoms were a pair of well used boys long-johns that were slightly too small for her. So, a child who wets the bed is not put on the toilet, a diaper is not put on her, the hair ties and jewellery are left on, the oversized underwear is left on, and the old long johns are put on while she sleeps.

Patsy recalls she left the bedroom door slightly open and went into the next room to do a bit more packing. She then left out some presents by the door for the garage (although in one interview John claims to have driven to the airport that day to drop off presents to take on the plane) while John and Burke worked on a model. I don't know if Patsy ever mentioned where she got these presents from. We know there were some in the basement. I also don't know where the presents went, as I cannot see any in the crime scene photographs. I don't know if any lights were left on anywhere in the house. Patsy then went up to bed. Again, there are slightly differing accounts as to whether John was already in bed or not.

The next morning Patsy gets up early and puts back on the clothes she wore the night before (why not pyjamas and dressing gown that she wore on Christmas morning?). I don't know if she changed her underwear from the night before. When she says she also put on make-up it would be interesting to know if it's the same as what she was wearing the night before. John does not see her do any of this. In a later interview she explains all this by saying her shower was broken and when she got up John was already using his shower. At approx. 5.30am, dressed in a red turtleneck sweater, black velvet trousers, and full make-up, she walks across the house and goes down the set of stairs near JonBenét's bedroom. She believes her door is in the same position as when she left it. She decides to rinse an item of JonBenét's clothing in the sink in the laundry area, no doubt leaving fresh fingerprints, then makes her way down the spiral staircase.

We know the account (s) of finding the ransom note and checking the bedroom and calling for John and going back down to use the phone to call police. There are now exactly seven minutes before they arrive. We can count off two of those minutes with Patsy ringing the Whites and the Fernie's, the people she had probably hugged the night before in the same clothes she was wearing now. There is no mention of Patsy reading the ransom note after phoning the police, or checking any rooms, running into the garage to see if the doors were open. There is no mention of her going outside to call her name, no mention of going to Burke's room to make sure her only son was OK. In those five minutes between hanging up the phone and the police arriving she must have sat silently on the spiral staircase waiting for salvation. Perhaps she needed a rest. She claimed to have stepped over the pieces of paper left on the spiral staircase on the way down. Anyone who has ever used a spiral staircase knows they can be difficult to manoeuvre. But Patsy steps over the papers onto the next available step, possibly a length of three feet, possibly in the dark, possibly half asleep, possibly in shoes. She turns to read the first few lines. She does not pick any of the papers up. Instead, she then jumps back up over the papers, again another three feet, this time upwards. She calls for John (but does not call for JonBenét), checks JonBenét's bedroom (but does not call for JonBenét, runs to the other side of the house to check if Burke is in his room (but does not call for JonBenét), then runs back across the house and goes down the spiral staircase, jumping over the step with the ransom note for the third time.

When police arrive the ransom note is on the floor, presumably where John had left it. Patsy says that Linda Hoffman has a key to the house, is desperate for money, and knows they are going away that morning: means, motive, opportunity. Although Patsy does not say Linda's handwriting matches that of the note. After that, Patsy seems to stay in the Sunroom (directly above the wine cellar) being comforted by friends. We never really see or hear from her again until her daughter is found. But even that is strange.

She was desperately waiting for a phone call from the kidnappers. Three hours after the kidnappers were supposed to call, Patsy is still in the sunroom, but does not seem to be asking any questions. Around 1pm Fleet White comes up from the basement shouting for someone to call an ambulance. Patsy, who is only twenty feet away, does not move or call out or get up to see what's happening. She also does not move when John comes up and places the body down in the hallway where John and Arndt confirm JonBenét is dead. She does not move when the body is moved into the living room near the Christmas tree, or when the rug and sweater are placed over the child. How long all of this takes I don't know, but it is surprising Patsy is not rushing to find out. She continues to wait in the sunroom. It is only after the Fernies and the Whites and the pastor have all gone into the next room to see what's happened does Patsy make her entrance. She hugs her daughter and wails as the pastor leads the congregation in prayer. People then move into a different room as the police and FBI arrive. Later that night when police go to give the Ramseys an update and to arrange for an interview the next day to answer a few questions, they are told that Patsy has taken medication and is in no fit state to be spoken to. Although she managed to go on television a week later, she would not be in any state to be interviewed by the police for another four months. Does this make her a killer?

Well, not quite. She is considered to be the main suspect to many people as she was officially the last person to see JonBenét alive, and officially the first person to realise she was missing. There are gaps in the timeline where both Patsy and John state that they were not in sight of each other, such as being in different rooms on Christmas night, going to bed at different times, and not seeing each other getting out of bed at different times. This may not look like much, but even asking John the simple question of "Did you see your wife get undressed/dressed", is something he is unable to answer.

One theory is that Patsy is with JonBenét on Christmas night and there was a toileting issue, and she wets the bed. Patsy, who has spent a long day trying to please everyone, who still needs to pack not only for Michigan but also for Florida, who is approaching her fortieth birthday, now has a child and a bed that needs to be changed. The marks on JonBenét's body, including the marks around the genital area, were caused by Patsy trying to control her daughter and then trying to clean her rather too harshly. It all seems possible so far, apart from two issues.

The first is the piece of pineapple found in JonBenét's stomach. Why does Patsy not say to police that when they came home JonBenét had a piece of pineapple and then went up to bed? And if Patsy knows the bowl of pineapple is significant, why doesn't she wash it up? Even if you don't believe the item in her stomach is pineapple, Patsy's failure to recall anything about the bowl is strange. Although there is a simple reason. If you look at a floorplan of the house you can see the breakfast room is set away from the hall and the spiral staircase, and the ransom note, and the kitchen containing the flashlight, and the stairs to the basement with a suitcase under the broken window. It's quite possible that the bowl was left on the table in the breakfast room because Patsy believed nothing had happened in there.

The next issue is the head injury. Even if you believe that this happened far closer to the time of death than the ninety-minute timeline that experts say, it still happened. Both the pineapple and the skull fracture are events that put an intruder being in the house for nearly an hour, and more importantly, put JonBenét being awake at least an hour before she died. If you say she could have died at midnight, then you are also saying she could have eaten the pineapple and received the head injury at 11pm. But how and why would Patsy hit her daughter? We could do a whole list of scenarios, but we are still left with the question of why Patsy would not call the police if this was the case.

I think this is where the marks on JonBenét's body are important. Six-year-old kids, hyped up on sugar and emotion, can be extremely difficult to control. Tired mothers who have been busy all day and are trying to get everything done for another long day in the morning, can easily lose their patience. Night time tantrums when a child doesn't want to use the bathroom or get changed or go to bed may lead to a parent chastising their child far more severely than what they would normally do. JonBenét gets marks around her neck and her genital area. There is blood. These injuries alone would lead to questions by the police if they went to hospital. Then she gets a fractured skull. She is now unconscious. Like the scenarios with John, the only reason an ambulance wasn't called when the head injury occurred was because if JonBenét had gone to the hospital in the middle of the night unconscious, her vital organs slowing down to a dangerous level where even her breathing may have to be done by ventilator, the police would most definitely arrest John, possibly even Patsy.

But I am still struggling a bit here to see why Patsy would do any of this. In one interview Patsy said that after recovering from stage 4 ovarian cancer, a child wetting the bed is not a major issue. Some people say that older children who wet the bed can be victims of sexual abuse and that soiling themselves is a way of trying to keep the offender from abusing them. But JonBenét had grown out of diapers, and only started wetting the bed again when

Patsy was in the later stages of her chemotherapy. I would be interested to know if at the same time JonBenét started wetting the bed again her mother had to wear adult diapers.

We also still don't know where in the house any of these injuries happened. For those who think Patsy was involved throughout, JonBenét's bedroom has to be the starting point. The room is a mess, with clothes and hairbands thrown everywhere, the curtains open, and JonBenét still having bands in her hair when she was found, all imply that JonBenét did not sleep in her bed. But this cannot all happen in silence. John and Burke were still downstairs making a model. But that head injury still doesn't seem right. I think that no matter what, even if Patsy had hit JonBenét with something, she still would have called for an ambulance. So, could Patsy have done everything that night alone?

All the injuries could have been done by a woman. She could have carried JonBenét down to the basement. She would know where the cord and duct tape were kept (she had possibly bought them less than a month ago). The paintbrush was hers and the knot didn't have to be made by an expert. Let's go further and say that inside the knot some fibres were found which matched Patsy's clothing. That could only happen if she tied the knot, or she had used the white cord previously while wearing the clothes she wore on Christmas night. To say they could have come from JonBenét's hair when the knot was tied seems a bit of a stretch. And then there is the white blanket and Barbie top. Knowing that the wine cellar floor was cold concrete rather than carpet, the parental instinct of not wanting to place your child on such a lifeless surface must have been a subconscious consideration. They have also decided to get JonBenét's favourite Barbie top and leave it in the wine cellar. This could not have been in the tumble dryer as it had drops of blood on it. But Patsy could have been solely involved from start to finish…almost.

It's the same problem with Burke. One thought is why would Patsy break the paintbrush. What possible difference could it make to her? And then we have the use of the broken paintbrush itself. The distance of the cord from the back of the neck to the knot on the paintbrush is seventeen inches. I don't know if Patsy's arm would have been long enough to have been able to hold the neck and pull on the garotte at the same time, meaning it is clearly not a torture device, or that somebody else may have been in the basement with her at the same time.

It's the same problem with this investigation and any unsolved crime. We always seem to overreach when dealing with circumstantial evidence. Things always seem slightly out of focus. The idea that Patsy is the only one in the house who could have carried out everything from start to finish sounds plausible; but it feels more possible if another person was involved as well. In truth all we are doing is inserting fictional fillers into the narrative. You don't know how A got to C, so you make up a B to get there. But this does not rule Patsy out. Patsy could have written the ransom note, even if someone else was dictating it to her.

And perhaps here is the best link to Patsy and her daughter's death. The first thing we should say is that for every police handwriting expert, Patsy and Team Ramsey hired their own expert. Patsy never wrote a handwriting sample in controlled conditions. The defence team had a copy of the ransom note, which Patsy could look at before she wrote anything.

Experts can say that handwriting analysis is based on many things, such as how the phrasing of certain words indicate the personality of the writer, or how sentences help create a picture of a person's emotional traits. But I think the writing in the ransom note looks like her writing. I can't get away from that similarity. It's not a proven fact; but when I look at the ransom note and some of Patsy's handwriting they look like the work of the same person.

There is a Youtube video where Patsy is shown certain letters from the ransom note and then shown a list of the same letters written by her. The letters are listed side by side, such as an *a*, and then another *a*. Patsy is asked if they look similar, she replies "No." She is then asked if she can identify which list of letters are her own writing; and again, she says "No". How can she say they are different and not identify her own writing? No doubt she had been told by her lawyer not to implicate herself in any way, but on the flip side, why would Patsy implicate herself by writing the ransom note in the first place? If she was going to write a ransom note, wouldn't there be two things that come to mind: 1, You would want the note to be a as short as possible; 2, You would want to write it in capitals and possibly even with your non writing hand to distance yourself as far as you could from being linked to the note.

The only answer I can think of is that writing in capital letters is more difficult to hide your real style if you were required to write them again. The ambidextrous Patsy may only have been able toto write cursive with her weaker hand. And perhaps the longer the note, the more she could make the reader believe it was an intruder. You had a husband who had broken into the home a few months before and none of the neighbours noticed. You had the story of the man who played Father Christmas and his daughter being abducted over twenty years ago. You had the housemaid who mentioned that it must be a worry that such an attractive daughter might be kidnapped. You could use links to John's past and his business to lead the police on a false trail. You just had to emphasise over and over again that no one in the house was involved. The only issue was that you had to spend hours cleaning the place of any forensic evidence that could link the death to you. Patsy, who had learned shorthand after graduating from university with a degree in journalism, was the only person who could cover her tracks well enough to make it look like an intruder. This could be an example of how she did it, but perhaps we will never know the reason why she did it.

Even after going through possible theories for an intruder, Burke, John and Patsy, there is still no clear picture of what happened that night and who had a hand in its design. The liquid jigsaw allows one theory to float up, and just when you try and attach it to the evidence, it sinks back down again. Patsy, John, and Burke can all point to a single piece of the investigation and claim they didn't do it. Chances are they would be right. The proof of beyond all reasonable doubt is never met. This allows the intruder theorists to reasonably claim that an outsider did it. In the end you can stand wherever you like to look at this crime and still not agree with the person next to you as to which theory was the most likely to be the truth. For all the complexities of this investigation there may be a simple answer as to why. Perhaps what it needed was someone on the inside to see what had happened that night.

Part Three.

Pulp Fiction.

Chapter 20

One Detective.

Do not believe that you alone can be right.

The man who thinks that,

The man who maintains that only he has the power

To reason correctly, the gift to speak, the soul—

A man like that, when you know him, turns out empty.

Sophocles, *Antigone.*

How does a detective gain where they are able to solve a murder? Perhaps they start their career dealing with minor offences such as thefts, low-level assaults, and jobs that turn out not to be a crime. The most common link with all these is to find evidence, and to learn when people might not be telling you the whole truth. The police officer becomes a detective. Apart from the uniform, the difference is they deal with more of the investigation: gathering more evidence, getting more statements, carrying out more interviews for more serious offences. The gathering of information remains the same. What many detectives also learn is a brutal truth about human nature, that even with the most morally repugnant crimes, good people will lie. They may lie for many reasons, and they may be so convincing that a detective might begin to wonder if the suspect is right and the officer has got it wrong. The answer is they just need to remember that the facts are what they are. People can lie from start to finish, but the facts will always be there.

With the death of JonBenét Ramsey we can go to the very extremes on all the theories of how she died. Let's have one theory and say that nearly everything that happened could have been done by her. All the injuries she had could have been self-inflicted, including the skull injury. She could have made the garotte and put it around her neck. No matter how crazy all this sounds, lets treat it as a possibility. But there is one simple fact which rules this theory out: JonBenét did not write that ransom note. That does not mean the writer was involved in every other aspect of what happened to JonBenét that night, but they knew something had happened. The ransom note probably rules out more theories than trying to solve this case by DNA.

Every detective involved in this case knew that whatever theory they looked at, the central focus had to be the ransom note. And there is something else which helps a detective solve any crime including murder: teamwork. Twelve people sitting in a room could all have different opinions, but all would agree that whoever wrote the ransom note was linked to JonBenét's death. If they worked together then just by a simple process of elimination, they should be able to come up with the correct theory.

Steve Thomas was a good detective. He had worked on numerous units in Colorado, although never as part of a murder investigation team. But he knew how to deal with forensic evidence and had taken cases to court. He was not one of the original officers who visited the scene in those first few hours, and as such he missed those details so important to any investigation. The smell of detergent on a carpet, the lack of underwear in the laundry basket, a bed that's not been slept in. He never saw how John and Patsy behaved before and after the body was found, or the size and colour of the marks on JonBenét's body. But he was able to see all the police reports, he was able to get statements from witnesses, he was able to visit the house when it was empty, and later he was involved in interviewing the Ramseys themselves. Again, we should clarify that there were significant witness interviews, where its extremely difficult to challenge the person about what they have said. Formally, the Ramseys were always treated as significant witnesses. They could volunteer to come in and be interviewed anytime (like Fleet White), or they could make excuses and avoid answering any questions. This left John and Patsy holding all the cards, and literally everything else. In order for them to come in and speak, the Ramsey Defence Team demanded unedited forensic reports, police documents, and witness statements. These were duly handed over.

Quite early in the investigation Steve Thomas saw Patsy as the main suspect. Patsy had behaved strangely from the moment she had phoned the police. The handwriting in the ramson note was very similar to various notes and letters taken from the house which were confirmed as Patsy's handwriting. And although she had managed to go on television just a week after her daughter's death, she avoided coming in to speak to police to give them information to help catch her daughter's killer. Tomorrow, tomorrow, and tomorrow, crept in a series of petty excuses as to why they were not able to be interviewed. It was not until four months after JonBenét's death that Patsy was finally interviewed. During that time she and her lawyer learnt exactly how much information the police had, but she still could not answer all the questions put to her. Even on basic questions such as what JonBenét was wearing, or who the flashlight belonged to, Patsy remained vague. Little wonder that Steve had a hunch something was wrong.

Part of his theory was that Patsy was frazzled after a few weeks of non-stop activity building up to Christmas. Then a Christmas day in which John had spent most of it out of the house while she had to get the kids ready for a party and pack two sets of luggage. The next day was a flight to Michigan to be with Johns other children for a few days and then flying back to get on a commercial flight to Florida for a Disney cruise as part of Patsy's 40th birthday celebrations. When they got home on Christmas night JonBenét was still awake. Patsy lets her have some pineapple as Burke and John go to another room to fix a model. Patsy takes JonBenét upstairs, then goes into the spare bedroom to pack. At some point JonBenét, who has refused to wear a diaper, wets her bed. Patsy now has a pile of washing to do. Steve believes the vaginal trauma in the autopsy report was a combination of chronic bedwetting and a form of chastisement. JonBenét then receives a skull injury so severe that she slips into a coma. Patsy could have called for an ambulance, but panics. How could she explain the marks around the vagina and the neck and the head injury if the police were called and JonBenét cannot tell them it was an accident. Patsy decides to make up a kidnap story. She, along with everyone else in the country, has no idea just how much this story would capture public interest.

Steve believes at this stage John and Burke are asleep. Patsy moves the body down to the basement. Either believing JonBenét is dead, or that she has slipped into such a deep coma she is unlikely to survive, Patsy creates the garotte. This is not to kill JonBenét, but to make it look like part of a kidnap gone wrong. She finishes by wrapping her daughter in a blanket and places her favourite Barbie top next to her, something the FBI believe only someone extremely close to the child would have done. Patsy returns upstairs to the kitchen and starts a ransom note which began with *'Mr. & Mrs. I'*. She then changes her mind and drafts the long ransom note which only includes John Ramsey. At this point it should be mentioned that police believe there were other attempts due to the number of pages torn out from her notepad.

Patsy does not go to bed. Staying in the same clothes from the night before, with the same make up and her hair still done. The morning starts with her finding the ransom note, but never picking it up. Searching the bedrooms, but never calling her name. Calling the police, only to avoid them for the rest of the day. She calls for John, avoiding having to touch the ransom note. She makes the phone call.

By the time the White's arrive they wouldn't be able to tell if she had been up all night or was simply distraught from the trauma of the last thirty minutes. Steve believes Patsy does not tell John what has really happened, but he suspects her because of the handwriting on the ransom note. He finds the body sometime between 10.30 and 11.30am. He remains quiet because he wants police to find JonBenét, but they don't. So, when Detective Arndt asks him to search the house from top to bottom, he takes Fleet White and goes straight to the basement. The body is found. Patsy waits in the next room until everyone has seen her dead child, and then finally comes in and hugs her daughter, but never asks how she died. This is what Steve Thomas believed happened on Christmas night and the next morning.

Steve Thomas had access to all the evidence. More importantly, he was there as new information came in which was checked and either verified or ruled out. Then he would look at the growing questions that the Ramseys refused to be interviewed about and would inform the D.A that certainly Patsy should be told to voluntarily come in and be interviewed or be arrested and then interviewed. Once in custody Patsy would still be entitled to legal representation and the right not to answer any questions, but she could be challenged on everything she had said so far, and everything she claimed not to remember. The police would also be able to speed the investigation up. The D.A. would now have a duty to sign off search warrants. The problem was that in a murder investigation where no one had been arrested in those first few weeks, the D.A. could decide who, where, and when an arrest could take place.

The D.A. may have felt the handwriting analysis was inconclusive, especially after the Ramsey Defence Team paid for their own expert to say there was only a partial chance that patsy had written the note. The phrase "chronic vaginal trauma" possibly indicated a male being involved. The fibres found in the cord, the clothes and under the duct tape, could all have been transferred by innocent means. But perhaps the main issue was that linking Patsy to the ransom note did not automatically link her to the injuries JonBenét received. If you arrest Patsy, you might never get John to give an interview, or even to suddenly claim he woke up in the night with Patsy asleep next to him, weakening the case even further.

There were other problems. Some of those in the District Attorney's office were very close to the Ramsey Defence Team. It felt as if information was being leaked back to them as soon as it became important. Expert witnesses paid for by the police were matched with more expensive expert witnesses paid for by Team Ramsey. There was also the media to deal with. Alex Hunter, the D.A. in charge, felt that he needed to control the publicity on a personal level. Some reporters were openly hinting that the Ramseys were involved. Hunter, who had seen the O.J. Simpson saga turn from tragedy into a circus, didn't want the same thing to happen to the death of a little girl. But trying to control the media was like trying to control sharks in a feeding frenzy by holding up a fish. And all these things were stalling the investigation. The clock was ticking. Months, and months, and months were now creeping by. Every day lessened the chance of Patsy being arrested. And in the end, she never was. And so, the question comes down to: was detective Steve Thomas right in wanting Patsy arrested?

Yes. Let's say the odds of your partial DNA profile being found on JonBenét's underwear are a million to one. Those who believe in the intruder theory would certainly want you arrested. But these are the same odds as someone breaking into Patsy's home, usings Patsy's notepad and pen, and writing a ransom note that not only has similar handwriting to Patsy, but it also has similar phrasing, and contains information that Patsy would know. Of all the million homes to break into that night, the intruder picked the one where their handwriting profile matched that of the person who lived there.

The way it should have been done would be to arrest her for hindering the investigation rather than for murder. She would then have been properly interviewed without being given all the police information in advance, have her handwriting subjected to proper scrutiny, and possibly even have a lie detector test. If anything, it would have finally helped prove her innocence. And ideally, this is what should have happened even without the threat of being arrested. Patsy should have been at that police station every week. If Fleet White came in nineteen times to speak to the police, she should have done it twenty times. But she never. And the D.A. never made that judgement call. Which raised another question that played on Steve Thomas' conscience, did the D.A. impair the course of justice?

Well…not quite. The Ramseys always did just enough to not be arrested. They claimed they helped police by giving them all the samples they wanted, such as handwriting, DNA, and fingerprints. Under state law it's an offence if you refuse to give them. They said they wanted to be interviewed, just not in a police station, and when they were ready. They kept changing the conditions for when they would give an interview, including how long it would take, that it could only be done one after the after, with a break in-between for John and Patsy to speak to each other. They wanted copies of all witness statements and police reports. They kept delaying being interviewed until all the forensic reports had been completed, all cctv records had been erased, and the memories of any possible witnesses had faded over time. The answers Patsy gave in her first interview four months after her daughter had died were vague enough to require a second one, which would not take place until nearly two years later.

Steve Thomas went on to resign from the police due to the D.A.'s failure to prosecute the Ramseys. He published a book, *JonBenét, Inside the Murder Investigation*. He is quite open in suspecting the Ramseys of being involved in their daughter's death, although I don't think he ever uses the word "Murder". As well as the ransom note linking Patsy, he also believed this was based on the numerous changes of the narrative within their initial accounts. It's a simple position of time and space. You can say to one officer you came home at a certain time and did several things, and then later change the time when speaking to a different officer. Or you keep the time and remember that you did something slightly different. But it's difficult for your memory to be out in both the time and what you were doing. To constantly change what time you came home, and also change what you did when you were in the house, would make even the least experienced detective suspicious.

There is also something else in his book. While making enquiries a few weeks later Steve Thomas spoke to John's daughter's boyfriend. He had turned up that day along with John's son and daughter. John took them out of the house away from the police. The boyfriend heard John say to his children that he had found JonBenét's body around eleven o'clock that morning. This was the time that John went missing from Det Arndt's sight. It also explains why John was to later say that he had gone down into the basement before 1pm but was not sure of the time. What we have to ask is if this is true, why did John not say anything to police. Could it be that he knew who was involved?

If you watch police video footage of the house, you will see at the bottom of the spiral staircase the desk where the notepad and pen was found. Nearby is another desk. On it is a piece of paper with a message written in felt tip pen which appears to be written by Patsy. The word *John* in this message looks very much like the word *John* at the end of the ransom note. On the floor next to the desk is a brown attaché, whether this attaché case would be considered adequate would be a matter for John and the kidnapper.

But the ransom note is not a confession. Its possible Patsy can be linked to more of the events in the house than John or Burke; but there is nothing you can hold up and say it proves beyond all reasonable doubt that Patsy was involved in her daughter's death. She had the means and the opportunity, but what was the motive? Not self-defence but perhaps self-preservation. This should also include willing to sacrifice some of your ideals to save someone you love. No matter how strong your faith is, there are many who would be willing to do something bad in the belief it is for a greater good.

Perhaps the biggest flaw in Steve Thomas' argument is that he believes the whole thing started from a bedwetting incident, but the facts show JonBenét urinated lying face down in the basement. This may have happened post death when her bladder emptied as vital organs and stomach muscles stopped; but it's difficult to see how she drank anything after supposedly wetting the bed earlier in the night and being hit on the head. This is not to argue Patsy is innocent, but if your starting point is based on a medical impossibility, I just can't see a D.A. believing that she carried out all these events alone to the point they would formulate a charge. Once you introduce an element of doubt in the picture, you let the stranger theory to come back into the frame.

Chapter 21

Two Detectives.

The past is never dead. It's not even past. All of us labor in webs spun long before we were born, webs of heredity and environment, of desire and consequence, of history and eternity. Haunted by wrong turns and roads not taken, we pursue images perceived as new but whose providence dates to the dim dramas of childhood, which are themselves but ripples of consequence echoing down the generations. The quotidian demands of life distract from this resonance of images and events, but some of us feel it always.

William Faulkner.

Lou Smit was a great detective. He had spent nearly thirty years in the job and had worked on numerous murder investigations. Although he had retired by 1997, he was assigned by the D.A. to help with this case. He looked at the crime from a different perspective. He believed that the intruder theory was not only possible, it was also probable. You had the ransom note, which he believed could not have been written after JonBenét had died. You had the open window with the suitcase underneath, which Lou believed a man could climb through. You had a child with injuries which he believed no parent could inflict. On this basis he went firmly against the other detectives on the case. For every issue they had with his intruder theory, he put forward a possible scenario to explain it.

The first was the ransom note. Everyone agreed it had been written in the house and had taken possibly thirty minutes to write. It does seem incredible that a stranger would have killed JonBenét and then written the ransom note. It also seems incredible for someone to have got in that night and spend all that time writing while John (who could have had a gun) or a neighbour (who could have called the police) might have seen or heard them before they had taken JonBenét out of her bedroom. Lou Smits theory was that the intruder had broken into the home while the Ramseys were at the Christmas Party, and during those couple of hours alone they have written the note. This gives the intruder plenty of time to write the three pages with a light on, and that the note was written while JonBenét is still alive. Smits' reasoning behind this is that he thinks the ransom note was written in a calm and rational manner; whereas if it was after JonBenét had been killed, there is no way anyone could write three pages because they would be so desperate to escape. This is because Smit can't get away from the fact the note could not have been written any faster, and that an intruder would not have killed JonBenét first, and then written the ransom note demanding money. The issue Smit now has is that he must now believe the intruder has broken into the home with a clear motive. This is a premeditated kidnap. So why didn't the intruder finish what they had been planning?

The kidnapper waits. The family come home. Luckily, they don't stay up late, John doesn't check the windows or put the alarm system on. The kidnapper then waits for possibly two hours somewhere in the house. They go into JonBenét's bedroom. They possibly use a stun gun to incapacitate her. This theory comes from the two sets of similar looking marks on her body looking like stun gun marks. The Ramseys do not own a stun gun, therefore it must have been the kidnapper. The issue here is that the marks have never been confirmed as coming from a stun gun. The pathologist who looked at them said they were abrasions. Stun guns leave electrical burns. And why would the kidnapper need to use a stun gun when they presumably have the white cord and duct tape with them to control a six-year-old girl?

The kidnapper takes JonBenét out of the bedroom, stopping to collect the white blanket from the laundry area and possibly the Barbie top. They carry JonBenét down the spiral staircase, possibly in the dark, unless of course they have a flashlight. They stop to place the three pages of the ransom note neatly on a step. But wait. They are carrying a child wrapped in a blanket. Do they put her down somewhere. Perhaps this is when she eats the piece of pineapple.

The issue of the kidnapper and the piece of pineapple that JonBenét had eaten that night is never really explained in the intruder theory. No one wants to say it must have been the kidnapper, and so the answer is flipped to say it wasn't really pineapple in her stomach. We may agree and say it might have been a different piece of fruit, but we can't change facts. She did eat something within two hours of dying. The clock is ticking. Every second in that home is a chance of getting caught.

Smit believes the kidnapper takes JonBenét down to the basement and puts her into the suitcase to try and escape; but for some reason (either she does not fit, or the suitcase cannot get through the window) the kidnapper then decides to change motive. Hang on. They could have been planning this for months. They have possibly been hiding in this house for over four hours. They have spent a lot of time writing out a ransom note filled with specific details, which shows an element of this being a coordinated crime. They have possibly brought with them all the tools to carry out a successful abduction. And they either have a getaway vehicle or live close enough for them to carry a child that distance without getting caught. This is all about financial gain. Surely, we are not saying this kidnapper's only chance of their plan coming together rested on the luck of the Ramsey's having a large suitcase in the basement and a window big enough for it to go through. Did they also think someone pulling a suitcase through the streets at two in the morning would look less conspicuous that someone carrying a white blanket? And now that the suitcase doesn't fit through the window (did anyone ever check?) Lou smit changes the kidnappers name, and from now on all those on the Ramsey defence team will refer to them as "The Intruder".

Even in the basement the clock is still ticking. Rather than escape, the intruder decides to spend more even time in the house. The reason is because Smit believes this is when the motive now becomes a sexual one. The garotte is created. JonBenét is strangled for the intruder's perverted pleasure. The issue with this is that the cord is pulled from the back of the neck, and the throat shows no internal injuries. The sexual motive also implies that the intruder (and killer) was a male. We know there is some form of vaginal trauma, but it's not rape. And if the intruder was carrying out some sort of sado-masochistic act, why does he not tie the cord around the neck and wrists far more tightly than what they were and shorten the length of the cord for him to be close to the body?

The intruder then hits the child on the head so hard it fractures her skull. The sexual motive now becomes a murderous one. Why the need to hit her is explained by Smit as a continuation of the sexual pleasure. But this makes no sense. The cord is seventeen inches long, and the strangulation was caused by her breathing becoming so shallow it eventually stopped rather than the tightening of the noose. Even if we dispute the autopsy report which shows that the skull injury happened prior to the strangulation, the cord around the neck is lateral, meaning the intruder is at the same height as JonBenét or directly above her when he caused the injury. If so, how do they cause the damage? Then we have the duct tape. Rather than it being put on while she was in the bedroom, it's believed that the tape was put over her mouth while she was unconscious or dead as there is no sign of JonBenét moving her jaw or struggling to breathe. If the intruder had brought along a roll of duct tape specifically to keep her quiet, it seems a bit of a waste to use it now. Let's also not forget that Smit uses the intruder theory to explain a neighbour hearing a scream sometime between one and two in the morning. Smit states that the attack took place in the boiler room next to the wine cellar. There is an air duct which would have sent the sound of the scream towards the neighbours but would not have been heard by John and Patsy at the top of the house. This is all fine, apart from the fact that Smit does not explain why JonBenét would be able to scream loud enough for someone across the street to hear, and only once. The intruder must be close enough to stop her from calling out, especially if they have put the garotte around her neck. The neighbour would later tell police she couldn't remember if the scream was on Christmas night or a few nights before. The final issue is that we don't know if it was JonBenét who screamed. A scream loud enough and short enough to be heard across the street could have been done by an adult female.

Once JonBenét had been carried into the wine cellar wrapped in the white blanket (she was not placed under it), and whatever was used to fracture her skull has been put away, the intruder continued to tidy up. The note pad and pen put back where they had come from. One end of the broken paint brush put back in the paintbrush tray. The stun gun, the ball of white cord, and the roll of duct tape are all taken away. The intruder even takes the time to clean down

JonBenét and putting away the cloth before dressing JonBenét in the large underwear and small long-johns. The clock is still ticking. But the intruder then looks around the basement, and rather than use the nearby chair or footstool, they use the suitcase to climb back out of the basement window. This raises another question; why didn't the intruder put the chair underneath the window when they tried to put the suitcase and Jonbenet through the window? They then feel the need to lower the heavy metallic grate after they have climbed out of the basement. Even though the suitcase and the open broken window is a tangible clue, the intruder manages not to leave any evidence, but its argued that not strictly true.

Unfortunately, the intruder allegedly leaves behind traces of their DNA under JonBenet's fingernails, on the oversized underwear and well used boys long-johns. As the DNA is either to weak or has been contaminated by other DNA cells, its origin is simply classified as "Unknown". How the intruder managed not to leave any DNA on her top, anywhere else on her body, the blanket, the duct tape, the cord, the ransom notes, the flashlight, the paintbrush, the bedroom and in the basement is a remarkable piece of luck. Let's not forget that all of this has taken somewhere between three to four hours, in the dark, in a house they do not know.

But the kidnapper/Intruder has been luckier than that. They were lucky the Ramseys did not fix the broken window, the dog had been taken to a neighbour's earlier that day, if they had turned up the next night no one would have been home, if they had a vehicle and were watching the house, they have not been seen by any of the neighbours. Lucky they have not left any footprints in the snow. They were very lucky that the house alarm was not turned on while the family were out. Lucky that John's other children had first not come to Boulder that night. They were lucky that the basement window did not have a bolt on it, the window had not been repaired and so had to make a noise trying to smash it open, that the games room and basement door did not have a lock. The intruder must have been lucky they were wearing gloves, as no unidentified fingerprints were found in the house, nor were any clothing fibres.

It seems that the only time they were unlucky was when JonBenét got traces of their DNA under her fingernails. Current tests show it's not skin cells or hair and could be a composite of at least two people. The kidnapper also somehow gets DNA on the old pair of boys long-johns and the underwear, which is also strange, as we don't know if they were the same items that JonBenét was wearing when she went to bed. We should also remember that the

DNA found under the fingernail does not match that found on the clothing. Perhaps there was more than one intruder?

Smit also believed that some dried leaves and packaging debris found in the wine cellar were the same as those in the weather grate. This may be true; but when is this meant to have happened? It can't be when the intruder first comes into the house. And if it was when they were trying to get JonBenét out, why is there no evidence of the same debris on the white blanket or her clothing?

If you add this scenario to the ever-growing list of strange circumstances, it becomes clear that the intruder theory only fits if you blur the edges of certain events. When police arrived, they saw JonBenét's bed sheet pulled back (although the intruder politely closed the door on their way out). They saw the ransom note on the floor next to the spiral staircase (that John and Patsy never seem to touch). They have the large black flashlight in the kitchen (that John and Patsy never decisively claim to own). There is the suitcase under the open broken window in the basement (that John and Patsy never say they moved). There is also the baseball bat outside with carpet fibres on it (another item John and Patsy cannot remember if it belongs to them). And now debris from the recess is found in the wine cellar. The only thing missing is a watch where the face had been broken at the (alleged) time of death. It all feels rather like the scene from *Murder on the Orient Express*, with Hercule Poirot realising 'There are too many clues.'

But perhaps the biggest flaw in the intruder theory is the DNA. Smit originally claimed that the DNA found on the pyjama bottoms, the underwear and under JonBenét's fingernail, were all the same. This was not true. The only thing that linked the three sets of DNA is that they have come from a male. This could be three different nine-year-old boys for all we know. The chances of finding a full profile are a million to one, just like matching the ransom note to someone. Cells interlinked within cells.

At least Lou Smits' theory allows the evidence to be put into some sort of chronological order and give reasons as to why they happened. But theory is not reality. For a start I feel that Smit focuses too much on the stun gun. There are no marks on JonBenét's white top. If a stun gun was used, they must have lifted the top to place the gun on her back. Why? And when would they have used it twice? Let's say the first time was in her bedroom. They then take her down into the basement, tape her mouth and tie her hands (but not her legs). Is it then they decide to use it again? There is simply no reason.

On another point, Smits has looked at the evidence and seen that there were marks around the neck which he believes indicated JonBenét was alive while the garrotte was wrapped around her neck. And these marks were scratches caused by JonBenét herself, which also indicate that her hands were not tied at this point. But the DNA under her fingernails shows no results of her own skin. So, Smit changes the narrative slightly. The intruder, halfway through a successful kidnapping, decides to carry out a sexual assault, and then a murder. But surely this is not how motives work? Smit negates the issue by saying that the intruder also had a hatred of John, and this was just as much a way of torturing him than JonBenét. This sounds like another motive. How many does this intruder need?

Smit firmly believed the ransom note was written before JonBenét died. I can understand his reasoning. If you are a parent and you have ever had to attend hospital because your child had been in an accident, would you be able to write a letter three pages long that wasn't filled with spelling mistakes, grammatical errors, and a writing style that would show you are under a lot of stress? It must be even more difficult if a loved one had suddenly died. Let's add into the mix that you have never been in trouble with the police before and the child's death could also link you to a crime. The fear that you might get caught, the shame of what your friends and family would say, the prospect of going to prison must have an effect. How do you write a three-page ransom note when every ounce of your body is screaming at you to escape? Perhaps the answer is you know you must take a different action because you cannot possibly escape from that house, or it must be done to stop another bad thing happening.

What I find different from Smits' theory more than anything is the language used. For a start, this isn't a kidnapper, a paedophile, someone who wanted revenge; this is an intruder. And an intruder can have many different motives. Perhaps even Lou was unsure as to what the main motive was. This lead sus to an issue with the language used. Whenever the intruder theory is discussed, words such as "Brutal", "Violent", and "Horrific" appear. The killer is a brutal psychopath who tortured a six-year-old girl for their own perverted needs, or, they were a violent horrific animal who does not think the same as normal people. This form of narrative gives someone looking at the investigation an element of doubt that a parent with no previous history of abuse could commit such a terrible act on their own child. But in many ways the brutality lies is in the images rather than the act itself. The pictures of the skull fracture are harsh; but go to any hospital and look at pictures of accidents and you will see similar injuries. The garotte is distressing, but there are no internal injuries to her neck, meaning it was never pulled tight. The duct tape over her mouth was put on when she wasn't moving. When she was found in the wine cellar, she was wrapped in the blanket rather than being hidden by it. This is not to take away the fact that the death of a child is always distressing, but it feels as though Smit has gone from a murder mystery to a horror.

Smit eventually resigned as an investigator from the Boulder Police department and went to work for the Ramsey Defence Team. A year later he gave an eight-hour presentation to the Grand Jury in relation to an intruder committing the crime. He must have felt vindicated when at the end the District Attorney publicly announced there would be no prosecution against anyone. Smit never knew that the jury had in fact decided that John and Patsy should be prosecuted. He couldn't convince a jury that there was enough of an element of reasonable doubt that the Ramseys were not involved.

Perhaps the most important thing about the intruder theory is that a great detective such as Lou Smit spent nearly thirteen years on just one investigation and still could not find a suspect before he passed away inn 2010. His family and colleagues have continued to carry on his work. They have still not been able to charge anyone.

So, who was right. The pathologist had mentioned that there had been chronic abuse top JonBenét's vagina. It was later believed that there had been an incident of some kind up to ten days before her death where JonBenét had suffered some sort of trauma. This may have been sexual, it may have been some form of punishment, it may have been self-inflicted. Both Thomas and Smit tend to avoid dealing with this. The marks on JonBenét's face and back are also avoided by Thomas. Smit tries to resolve the issue by introducing a stun gun, but there is no proof of this. Thomas believes the garotte is staged, Smit believes it is part of a sexual act. I have to go with Thomas on this one due to the lack of injuries on JonBenét's neck. Neither can explain why someone would put JonBenét in the wine cellar and locked the door. But again, I have to go with Thomas, if only because it makes absolutely no sense for the person who wrote the ransom note to leave the body behind. And on the balance of probabilities, I am going to go with Steve Thomas. But in a criminal trial the burden of proof must be beyond all reasonable doubt.

Chapter 22

Witness to the Prosecution.

What is the price of lies? Not that we confuse them with the truth. The real danger is that we have heard so many of those lies that we no longer recognize the truth. What to do then? All that remains is to abandon even the idea of truth and be satisfied with stories. In these stories it doesn't matter who the heroes are. What we want to know is who to blame.

Valerij Alekseevič Legasov – *when giving evidence in relation to the Chernobyl nuclear disaster of 1986.*

For all the mistakes made by police from 5.52 am on the 26th of December, they were nothing compared to the bad decisions that continued to be made by the District Attorney's Office. From day one, those officers dealing with the investigation also found themselves hindered by their own prosecution team. In the morning they were told not to look too deep into the Ramsey's, and then put on radio silence. Warrants were delayed or refused, important lines of enquiry were stopped, circumstantial information was ordered to be investigated, and no one in the District Attorney's Office seemed to be interested in making an arrest.

Even worse, within a matter of days the Ramseys had a defence team that included a publicity agent, their own private detectives, and the best lawyers in Colorado, some of whom were former district attorneys and still had friends in office. Whenever the police wanted to speak to them, the Ramsey's would go on television to give their version of events. Whenever the police went to speak to an important witness, they found that the Ramsey Defence Team already had already been and got statements, which they refused to disclose. I suppose it comes down to whether you believe the Ramseys had been treated so appallingly, or rather, the police had dealt with the investigation so abysmally that they had lost all trust with the criminal justice system. But it still comes down to the fact that the police could not investigate this crime properly until they had learnt everything from the last two people to see JonBenét alive. Here is a brief summary of events.

26th December 1996. Police ask John and Patsy to come in as soon as possible to conduct significant witness interviews to help gather information. They are told Patsy was in no fit state, and the Ramseys would let them know.

1st January 1997. John and Patsy interviewed on television the day after burying their daughter. Patsy tells viewers to keep their children safe as there is a killer on the loose. The Ramseys never go back to the house. Instead, they move on numerous occasions. It should be said that they were now being followed by the media. The police continued to request an interview. After the Ramseys received a 1st generation photocopy of the ransom note in mid-April, they agreed to have their first interview, but did not want to do it at a police station.

30th April 1997. John and Patsy interviewed for first time at Boulder District Attorney's office.

1st May 1997. John and Patsy give interview to the press, with all questions set out beforehand. In it they gave a statement declaring their innocence.

Nothing seems to happen for another year. The police continue to ask for further interviews but get no response. At the start of June 1998 there are reports the Governor of Colorado wants to set up a Grand Jury to find out if there is enough evidence to charge anyone with JonBenét's death.

23rd June 1998. John and Patsy interviewed by police for the second time.

September 1998. Grand Jury convenes. It is essentially a trial without any defendants.

13th October 1999. D.A. Alex Hunter appears outside the court to tell the press that no indictments would be made due to lack of evidence. This would later be found to be incorrect.

17th March 2000. John and Patsy interviewed on television by Barbara Walters in relation to their book, *The Death of Innocence*.

21st May 2000. John and Patsy interviewed by Larry king. They are joined by former detective Steve Thomas. It is a live broadcast. He openly accuses them of being involved in their daughters death.

29th August 2000. John and Patsy interviewed by the police for the third and final time.

The Police Interviews

How cooperative were the Ramseys? Not giving interviews when you are not a suspect is not an offence, but for many it was their unwillingness to cooperate that was the issue. The difficulty for the police in this situation is that the last thing they wanted was for the Ramseys to write a statement declaring their innocence and then refuse to speak. To be fair, after a few months it didn't really matter. If all the evidence was in the house that night, and the police could not link the Ramseys to the death of their daughter, then the game was over. If the Ramseys kept to their story, the police would find it impossible to charge. Stick to JonBenét being asleep when they got home and finding the ransom note when you woke up. That pushes you out of the window of opportunity. Point to the ransom note as the intruder's motive. And the suitcase under the basement window was their means to carry out the crime. Anything else, just give vague answers. By April 1997, the only way they would now be arrested would be if DNA technology found new evidence, or a Grand Jury believed there was already enough evidence to have them charged.

Patsy.

1st account taken on 26th December 1996.

Officer French puts in his report that Patsy told him that JonBenét had been put to bed dressed in white pyjama bottoms and a red turtleneck top when she was put to bed. In the morning Patsy checked JonBenét's bedroom and could not see her. She washed an item of clothing then went down the stairs, saw the ransom note and immediately called the police.

First police interview, 30th April 1997.

Patsy states that there were presents in the wine cellar which they were going to take to Michigan. There were also presents in the wine cellar for Burke's birthday a few weeks later. She was last in the basement on Christmas day wrapping presents (does this mean she went into the wine cellar as well?) but cannot recall the exact time. John put some of the presents in the Jeep later that afternoon. It's not clear if these are the presents for Michigan or the neighbours Patsy would drop off that night. They attend the White's party, leaving between 8 and 9pm. JonBenét fell asleep in the car and was carried up to bed by John. Patsy changed remembers she changed JonBenét's pants for a pair of pyjama bottoms while Burke and John played with a toy (she cannot remember where in the house). From now on she claims to never see or speak to John and Burke until the morning, and even then, its only to John after she finds the ransom note. Patsy then finishes packing and puts some presents by the back door before she goes to bed (I don't know if she has gone down to the wine cellar to get these while still wearing the same clothes she would put on the next morning, but this new comment also allows for any of her clothing fibres that had been found to now have an innocent explanation). Patsy then goes to bed between 9.30 – 10pm. She does not know what time Burke and John go to bed.

The next day she gets up at 5.30am while John is in the shower. She puts on the same clothes from the night before and puts on make-up. They are due to be at the airport for 6.30 - 7am. Patsy goes downstairs to the laundry area by JonBenét's bedroom and cleans a red jumpsuit belonging to JonBenét. She then goes down the spiral staircase and sees the ransom note. She only reads the first few lines before she runs up and opens JonBenét's bedroom door. She does not go in and search the room, instead she screams for John. He comes down from their bedroom just in his underwear (not known which set of stairs he uses). She tells him that JonBenét has been kidnapped. He tells her to call the police, then goes and checks on Burke. Burke, who is in the same floor as Patsy and has no idea of what's happening, does not come out of his bedroom after he hears his mother calling for his father. Patsy goes down the spiral staircase and waits for John. He comes down, takes the ransom note off the stairs and reads it. He tells her to call the police. She does, and then calls the Whites and the Fernies to tell them what's happened.

After the phone calls, Patsy believed that John checked the doors and windows (still in his boxer shorts, like what he was wearing when he broke the basement window a few months prior) before the police arrived.

When asked about the ransom demand of $118k being the same as Johns Christmas bonus, Patsy claims she had no idea how much he got, but thinks he may have said something about it being so similar on the morning of the 26th. When asked if she can recall anything being taken by the kidnapper, Patsy replies she doesn't know as she has never been back to the house in the last four months. She went on to say the basement window was broken in the summer when she and the children were in Michigan. When she gets back, she and the housemaid Linda Hoffman cleaned up the broken glass, but Patsy doesn't know why the glass pane is never replaced. She thinks Linda's husband was going to fix it. Patsy doesn't recall ever having duct tape or white cord in the house (but it's not known if she was asked if she bought those same items last December). When shown a picture of the blue suitcase she believed it belonged to Johns eldest son but doesn't recall whereabouts in the basement it would have been stored.

Second police interview, June 1998.

Patsy states she spent about twenty minutes putting on her make up on the morning of the 26th (while John was in the shower all this time?). When she came downstairs, she noticed JonBenét's door was slightly ajar, the same position she had left it the night before. She spends about ten minutes in the laundry area cleaning a red jumpsuit. She clarifies to police interviewing her that they didn't really need suitcases for the trip to Michigan as they already had clothes there, and the bin bag full of clothes that had been seen at the bottom of the spiral staircase and then moved by someone later that day could have been what they were taking to Michigan.

She repeated the order of events from finding the note to the police arriving, which highlighted an interesting point: There appears to be no conversation with John after she calls the police. Neither asks about the ransom note or what the police have said. She simply phones the Whites and the Fernie's and asks them to come over. Then she and John say nothing until police arrive. Patsy goes on to explain why the friendship with the Whites stopped. Fleet started acting strangely on that day and Priscilla White seemed to know more than what she was letting on. Strange, as the Whites had a rock-solid alibi of numerous witnesses being with them until about 2am on Christmas night.

When asked about the oversized underwear, Patsy said that JonBenét did have underwear with days on the week on them but cannot explain why the ones Jonbenet was wearing when found were twice the size she normally wore. Patsy is shown a photograph of JonBenét's bedroom and points out a pink pyjama set that JonBenét wore on Christmas eve. The reason Patsy didn't put these on JonBenét on Christmas night was because they must have been under the pillow, and she didn't see them. When shown a picture of the red turtleneck sweater that JonBenét was supposed to wear at the party crumpled in the corner of the bathroom, the one that she told police on the 26th that JonBenét had gone to bed wearing, Patsy doesn't know it got there, and starts to cry (why would this item create such an emotion eighteen months later?). Its not clear to me if this red top is the same red top that Patsy said she had washed earlier that morning (possibly leaving red fibres not only in the sink but also on her own clothing).

In relation to the presents in the wine cellar being partially unwrapped, she believes that she did it as they were delivered wrapped and she wanted to check what was inside. When asked about the glass of iced tea, the pineapple, and the box of tissues on the breakfast table, Patsy does not know how the box of tissues got there and is not even sure the box of tissues is even hers (This feels a bit like trying to divert the conversation away from the pineapple; and are we really going to believe the intruder brought a flashlight and a box of tissues with them?). She tells police that neither Burke nor JonBenét would have gotten up in the night to make themselves a snack. Patsy admitted she had bought fresh pineapple before Christmas and there would have been some in the fridge. She is shown a picture of a black baseball bat and asked if it would be stored in the basement. She replies that she doesn't know who it belongs to, but things like that would usually be stored in the garage.

There are two photographs of the spare bedroom next to JonBenét's. One shows a notepad on the desk, a white bin bag of clothes, and a bottle of cleaning fluid in the background. When it is pointed out to Patsy, she finds this strange, as the cleaning fluid is usually stored under the kitchen sink. The detective then tells her that photograph without those objects was taken by police when the house was a crime scene that day, the other photograph with the notepad, cleaning fluid, and bin bag of clothes was taken from the roll of film on the Ramseys own camera. Patsy cannot account for why anyone would take a picture of the spare room with cleaning fluid in the background. There are lots of notepads in the house, and the bin bag was probably moved to the bottom of the staircase at some point. Patsy then thinks she may have been carrying the bin bag of clothes that morning when she saw the ransom note and perhaps dropped the bag. As well as pictures of Christmas morning on the same roll of film, there is picture of the notepad on the desk near the spiral staircase. Patsy has no idea who took that photograph, or why. (It is not clear if this notepad is the same one from the spare bedroom, or the one that the ransom note was written.)

By the time we get to the third interview a Grand Jury had sat for over a year listening to all the evidence. Unknown to the public, the jury voted to charge John and Patsy and have a criminal trial, but Alex Hunter, came out of court and made a public announcement that there was not enough evidence to charge anyone with any offences relating to the death of JonBenét Ramsey. This was blatantly wrong, but it meant the Ramsey's would never face a criminal trial. There is no point going through the third and final interview. Its another series of vague answer, and to be honest, it feels a bit as a way for the Ramseys to push the intruder narrative.

Burke Interviews.

There are reports that when Burke was spoken to on the afternoon of the 26th December in the presence of an adult who was not a parent or guardian, he told a detective that after the party JonBenét did fall asleep in the car but woke up to help carry presents to a friend's house. When they got home, JonBenét walked in and went up the spiral stairs just ahead of Patsy. Burke and John played with a toy for a while and then he went to bed. He thinks he heard voices in the night but didn't know if it was a dream or not. The fact that he cannot remember the dream but believes he hears voices is very interesting. The adult who was present was Priscilla White's sister. Without the parents' permission, this conversation was deemed inadmissible and could never be used as evidence.

Burke is first officially spoken to in January 1997, two weeks after his sister had died. It was with a child psychologist. He was finally spoken to by police in June 1998 when it was proposed he might have to give evidence to the Grand Jury. I would say that no great revelations come out of these interviews. He went into his bedroom within thirty minutes of arriving home, he slept through the night, and was then escorted out of his bedroom and taken to a friend's house the next morning. It was argued that he had been trained to stick to a script, especially as the ten-year-old would sometimes answer with the line, "not that I recall". He was called to give evidence by the Grand Jury. It is not known what he said while giving evidence.

We have previously mentioned the murder of James Bulger in England in 1993. The two ten-year-old boys were identified and interviewed separately in the presence of a parent and a lawyer. In every interview the boys lied. When confronted with evidence the boys made partial admissions, blaming the other boy, then continued to lie. Even in the last interview when all the forensic evidence, the CCTV, the statements from witnesses, showed their involvement in James Bulgers death, each boy continued to lie and blame the other one. What this shows is that children can lie even about the most serious things. But we should also remember that these two boys had been brought up in neglected homes in which lying to the authorities, claiming benefits, showing no respect to the police, a parent never taking an interest in a child's education or welfare, created feral kids who didn't care about society and were incapable of remorse. Burke was raised with Christian values. He was raised to be respectful. He believed he had a sense of belonging within the community of Boulder. And let's not forget that here was a boy who had lost an older stepsister to a car accident, who had been told that his own mother could die of cancer and had lost his younger sister to a suspicious death, all before he was ten. He then spent the next twenty years within the shadow of that dark space between fame and infamy. Could anyone have survived that long trying to keep such a terrible secret? The recordings of his interviews as a child are difficult to analyse. How many other children are asked about their sister's murder? I don't think he was trying to evade psychologists or the police when they ask pertinent questions. I think his parents had told him to be careful when asking questions about certain things, and that is just what he does.

Perhaps it not until 2016 when he goes on the Dr Phil show (just before the CBC documentary which basically accused him of killing JonBenét) to give his version of events that we finally get his account. But again, he would have been coached about how to answer questions, about how his non-verbal communication would be judged, and no doubt would have sat with his lawyer going through what he would and would not say. And in the end, he pretty much doesn't say anything. Is this a sign of innocence? It's pretty hard to say.

Chapter 23

You Talking to Me?

When you have something to say, silence is a lie.

Jordan Peterson.

John Ramsey

1st accounts taken 26th December 1996

Officer French wrote his report that when he first arrived at the house he spoke to John, who told him that they had arrived home around 10pm, and he had read to both children for a short time, and everyone was in bed by 10.30pm.

Detective Arndt stated that when he spoke to John on that day, he told her that he read a book to JonBenét, tucked her into bed, then he went to bed.

John was to later say that both officers were wrong.

Johns first interview, April 30th, 1997.

John stated that at lunchtime Christmas day he went to the airport to put the Christmas presents into the plane. He mentions that Patsy didn't really want to go, but Burke wanted to spend time in Michigan. They spent a few hours at Fleet White's party, and they got home about nine-ish. JonBenet had fallen fast to sleep so he carried her upstairs and put her in bed. He then went down to help Burke with a toy for 10 to 15 minutes. They then went to bed as Burke knew they had to get up early. John then went upstairs and got ready for bed himself. He took a sleeping pill and read for a little bit until around ten-thirty. That's about an hour. He doesn't remember if Patsy was in bed by then (he appears to have had no contact with her since they arrived home ninety minutes ago). He slept soundly.

He woke up just before 5.30am and while Patsy was still in bed, he took a shower (I am assuming she is still asleep and it's still dark). He was getting dressed when he heard Patsy scream (Patsy has spent over twenty minutes getting washed and dressed, putting on make-up and cleaning an item of clothing, and this is their first contact of the day). He ran downstairs, and Patsy showed him the note. He then corrects himself and says he thinks he met Patsy as she came up the spiral staircase (I thought she had checked JonBenét's bedroom?). He then goes down and sees the note (still on the stairs). He places the note on the floor and reads it while Patsy calls the police. At some point he goes to check on Burke, who appears to be sleeping (John doesn't wake him up to ask if he has seen his sister).

He remembers getting Burke up later that morning and someone taking him away, but cannot recall saying anything. He also remembers going down into the basement (time not known) and seeing the broken window was open (with the suitcase directly underneath), so he latched it. Later, at around 1pm he and Fleet White were asked to search the house and they went to the wine cellar. He remembers finding JonBenét wrapped in the blanket.

Police went back to the basement window. John tells them that he broke it in the summer. He removed the weather grate from the wall to get down into the recess. He took his suit and trousers off before he climbed down. He kicked the glass pane out and climbed in feet first wearing just his boxer shorts. He believes Patsy asked the housemaids husband to repair the window around Thanksgiving. On the morning of the 26th of December, he found it a little odd that the broken window was open but doesn't tell anyone. John changes the subject to say that the housemaid had been acting strangely before Christmas (how many times had he met her?). When asked if he would take a polygraph test, John replies that he finds the idea insulting.

There are no real questions or challenges to John at this stage. What is also missing are detailed questions where we could trace Johns every step, and every thought or word in each moment. This is the issue with all these interviews. Detectives may have suspected something was wrong, but they couldn't treat John as a suspect. John knew the police were relying on him as a significant witness, they would never know if he was an unreliable narrator.

Second Interview, June 1998

This interview took place after Patsy's, with a break in-between, as per their request, for them to be able to speak to each other. This pretty much rules out knowing if John was recalling from memory, or remembering a script that Patsy had just said.

John believed JonBenét, Burke and Patsy got a bike on Christmas Day (I thought Burke was getting a bike for his birthday?). JonBenét also got a life size lookalike doll. There were a few more presents that had been wrapped for Burke and JonBenét for when they got to Michigan. John thinks he wrapped some of these presents on Christmas day (in the basement?) but cannot remember if he went into the wine cellar that day. Some children then come over to play (he does not mention going to the airport). The family go to the party, come home, and go to bed.

In the morning he thinks that Patsy handed him the note either on the landing or the spiral staircase. He does not read anything until he is on the ground floor. Patsy calls the police, then the Whites, then the Fernies (why does he stay for these calls rather than search the house?). John then says that they both checked JonBenet's bedroom and probably Burke's room. They then go back downstairs, and Patsy calls the police. He then remembers Patsy calls her two friends (he must be confused over the order of events, and he is still in his underwear at this point). He then goes up the two flights of stairs to get dressed. A short time later he comes back down to look through the house (but not the basement) before the police arrive (which must be within a minute).

Although quite a bit of time has passed, it seems strange that John seems to have forgotten so much, or cannot recall the order of events. There could be many reasons for this. It may just be age and time. It may be that he cannot genuinely the story he had given in the previous interview. It may be something Patsy has told him just before this interview, and it is overriding his thought process.

John remembers going back down into the basement with Fleet White. He gives details of seeing JonBenét wrapped in the blanket, "It looked like somebody was trying to make her comfortable, because it was under her, completely under her head and brought up around her". John could see the duct tape over the mouth. He tried to loosen the ties around her wrists before taking her out of the blanket and carrying her upstairs (why not the cord around her neck as well?). John is shown photographs of the bowl of pineapple. He comments that the kids like pineapple but doesn't think they would use that bowl or spoon, certainly not with iced tea. Police go back to the basement window.

In the summer of 96 John has got home about 11.30pm and realised he has forgotten his keys. Patsy was out. He lifted the grill off then kicked in the glass pane. He took his suit off and climbed in by turning around so that his knees were on the windowsill and then jumping down backwards so that he is facing the wall (leaving a scuff mark?). You could argue that breaking in at night allows him not to call any friends for a spare key, but there should also be a clear set of John's fingerprints on the windowsill and possibly even some auxiliary hair from his arms or legs.

When shown a photograph of the suitcase, John comments that when he first saw it in the morning it was flat against the wall rather than sticking out. This is the first time he has ever mentioned such an important piece of information. Some have argued that this feels as though this is more like an attempt to change the narrative than tell the truth. After 18 months of the public pointing out the strangeness of someone trying to climb out of the window with a suitcase in such a bizarre position, he simply now remembers it was flat against the wall, and he moved it so that it now sticks out. He claims he moved the case to look for pieces of glass (that he broke from the window a few months ago?), which he found, and may have put them on the windowsill or on the suitcase itself.

John is shown pictures of the basement. He does not know why his cigar box has been moved, nor why some of the presents in the wine cellar have been partially unwrapped. In the doorframe of the games room door is a chair, which John had to move out of the way to get into the games room (implying the intruder had to turn and place it across the door on their way out, although neither officer French nor Fleet White mention a chair blocking the doorway).

John is shown a picture of the flashlight in the kitchen. He states it could be his, but he's not sure as it looks a little bigger than the flashlight that he thinks is in the house somewhere. When asked if he put it in the kitchen John replies, "Not that I recall". When asked if he used a flashlight to search for JonBenét that morning, he replies, "I don't think so."

John is asked about the ransom note and if there was any conversation before the phone call about not calling the police. John replies that there was. Patsy told him the ransom note says not to call the police (this is strange, as the order not to contact the police is halfway down the second page of the ransom note, and Patsy claimed to have only ever read the first few lines of the first page), but John replies to call them anyway.

There are further questions about some of the pictures taken with the Ramsey's camera. The roll of film contains a picture of the note pad. John replies that he may have accidentally clicked the button when he was checking the camera. There are also pictures of some plastic bags at the bottom of the spiral staircase which are not in the crime scene photos taken later that day by police. John can only say that "Sometimes when we bag up clothes that we were going to give away, you know, that might have been what that was..." he seems to think of something. John then remembers the police asked him for a picture of JonBenét, and he probably took some pictures that morning to use up the roll of film (I don't know if this was ever checked by looking at the sequence of pictures on the negative strips). Its strange how in this interview the stuff they had previously discussed seems to have faded from John's memory; but these new questions John is able to recall instantly.

John is shown photos of a grey baseball bat, and believes it is Burke's. He is then shown photos of a black baseball bat (the one that has the basement carpet fibres on it) and doesn't recall if it is Burke's, or why it was found in that area outside the house. John is asked if he is willing to give police permission to have access to personal information such as bank and phone records, rather than go through the process of obtaining a warrant. At this point John's solicitor steps in and asks that all requests could be granted if the police can give a reason why they want them. It should be noted that around the same time as this interview a decision was being made to set up a grand Jury to assess the investigation. And so, after only two interviews in nearly two years, the Ramseys effectively stopped talking to the police. There would be a final interview, which the Ramseys wanted to do before they were taken to civil court after claiming someone was a possible suspect for their daughter's death.

For the police there were a lot of questions that had been left unanswered. We still don't have a full timeline of events. The most obvious missing piece of the jigsaw is what John does between 10.30am and 12pm on the morning of the 26th. Even if he had gone down into the basement to move the suitcase and then collected the post, it would `not take ninety minutes to complete. I would also ask questions about where else he went in the basement that morning. He said he went into the games room, but then why not check the boiler room while he was there? If he had he might have noticed the smell of urine from the stain on the carpet. He might have also seen his cigar box has been moved, something he missed when he went back down with Fleet White.

After the D.A. claimed that there would be no trial in 1999, giving the implication the Ramseys were innocent, John and Patsy wrote a book, essentially giving the details account of what happened that the police had been trying to get for the last four years. But not everything goes to plan. To publicise *The death of Innocence*, they went on the Larry King Show on two occasions in the year 2000. During the first live broadcast members of the public called in with questions. On the second broadcast Steve Thomas came on to discuss the investigation. It's the first time the Ramseys ever appeared flustered. If this was a police suspect interview, their lawyer would have asked them to use their right to remain silent. Asked on television if they were willing to take a lie detector test, the Ramsey's answer was yes, but they wanted it done by a professional. They also never gave a date of when they were willing to do it. I believe that sometime later they took their own tests, carried out by their own experts, which were resulted as "inconclusive".

The investigation into JonBenét has continued to grow alongside the expansion of the internet and social media. Cells interlinked within cells. But what is missing are all the statements from police and witnesses. Some of these statements could be held in until someone is charged and taken to court. The Ramsey Defence Team could argue that any statement released into the public domain would irrevocably damage any trial, and as such have them blocked from being published. Statements from people such as the Stines, the White's, and the Fernies, in relation to Christmas night and what time the Ramseys left. Statements of JonBenét bringing presents up to their homes or being asleep in the car, and the Ramseys behaviour the next morning, should make no difference if an intruder committed the crime, but these statements have never been disclosed to the public.

Fleet White was interviewed eighteen times. These were all voluntary. He wanted to help. It would certainly be interesting to know what happened when he went into the basement and the wine cellar for the first time and if he ever told John about it before they went back down at 1pm. The housemaid Linda Hoffman was interviewed within 48hrs of JonBenét being found. She and her husband gave hair and handwriting samples and an account of her whereabouts on Christmas night. The most interesting question would be if she ever recognised the writing in the ransom note. But that's not the only issue. On one occasion the police showed Linda photographs of the crime scene, including those of JonBenét's bedroom. Linda pointed out that the Beauty and the Beast bed set was not the set she had put on the last time she was in the house just before Christmas day. This could mean that on Christmas night JonBenét's bedding must have been changed less than twenty-four hours before JonBenét died. The problem was detectives were showing Linda Hoffman crime scene pictures two years after JonBenet had died.

Things could have been so much different if she had been shown the pictures weeks, even months after. The fact that this never happened was a failing by the police. Linda also claimed that soon after JonBenét's death she was stopped from speaking to the media by the District Attorney and also the Ramsey Defence Team with the threat of being arrested and put in prison if she spoke before any trial was conducted. The fact that this happened was a failing by the American judicial system. She was not the only one. The police controller who answered the call from Patsy was also subpoenaed. She was told not to speak to anyone until she had given evidence otherwise she could be arrested. For twenty years she remained silent. Detective Linda Arndt resigned from the police because she felt she had been made a scapegoat for many of mistakes made that morning. The first thing she got when she left was a gagging order, making her unable to discuss the investigation outside of a court. How many others were told to keep quiet from fear of arrest and imprisonment I don't know.

And we are now entering the point when fact and fiction were becoming so intwined that people were beginning to lose track of what actually happened. In 2000 in relation to a civil trial, Patsy was questioned about the ransom note and her own handwriting. One question was if she could recognise her own handwriting from the ransom note, to which she said *No*. I would suggest most people can recognise their own writing. Patsy was shown a few words that had been written under a photograph of JonBenét and asked if it was her handwriting; she said she couldn't recall. She was then shown individual letters from both her handwriting, and the ransom note, and asked if there was any similarity between them, to which she replied "No." Of course, it could be argued that Patsy had taken legal advice and had no choice but to deny everything, even recognising her own signature. John also could not identify Patsy's handwriting from the ransom note. He then says Patsy could not have written the ransom note due to the number of spelling mistakes (two). Even when shown photographs of JonBenét with Patsy's writing next to it, he fails to identify her handwriting. This again may be advice from his legal team to never admit any links between them and the ransom note. It also shows that within four years both sides were dealing with evidence within copies of copies of copies, almost forgetting a real child had died.

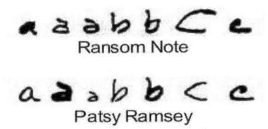

Ransom Note

Patsy Ramsey

Chapter 24

Sometimes things gain a momentum
Of their own.

I want to say one thing to the American people. I want you to listen to me. I'm going to say this again: I did not have sexual relations with that woman, Miss Lewinsky. I never told anybody to lie. Not a single time. Never. These allegations are false.

President Bill Clinton, *January 26th, 1998.*

Indeed, I did have a relationship with Miss Lewinsky that was not appropriate. In fact, it was wrong. It constituted a critical lapse in judgment and a personal failure on my part for which I am solely and completely responsible. But I told the grand jury today and I say to you now, that at no time did I ask anyone to lie, to hide or destroy evidence or to take any other unlawful action.

President Bill Clinton, *August 17th 1998, after DNA taken from semen on Miss Lewinsky's dress was confirmed to be his.*

There were stories that everything would collapse at midnight on the last day of 1999. Computers would not cope as millions of cells tried to transition from one century to another. The world needed strong leaders to tell them the truth. Two years prior to the millennium President Bill Clinton went on television to assure the American public that he had not had sexual relations with another woman. A few months later when the evidence was overwhelming, he went back on television to tell the public that he had been mistaken. The words he had used perhaps were not as clear as what he wanted to express. In truth, he had lied, but he and his team constantly used other words to hide this fact. It showed viewers two things; the first is that those at the very top were willing to lie with impunity to protect themselves, and the second is that language could be manipulated to mean whatever you wanted it to mean. There was also something else that happened around this time. Libel and defamation laws, very closely controlled in the old media of press and television, didn't seem to apply to the internet. If enough people believed your opinion it was treated as a fact.

The closest thing to the JonBenét investigation in terms of public interest was the disappearance of Madeleine McCann. In May 2007 the three-year-old English girl was holidaying in Portugal with her parents and her younger twin siblings. While her parents spent an evening in the nearby tapas bar with friends, the three children were left alone in their villa, with someone in the group checking them on a regular basis. At some point Madeleine's mother checked the villa and realised her daughter was missing. The police are called, a search is made. There are issues with the police not protecting the crime scene properly at the very start. There is a damaged window, and a report of a male seen on the night, possibly carrying a child, although nothing is ever confirmed.

Police finally speak to Mr and Mrs McCann a few months later in September, as witnesses. And a day later listed them as suspects. The McCann's, who both worked in the medical profession, flew home. They later appear in the media saying they believed their apartment was being watched. A year after Portuguese police fly to England to interview the McCanns again. Mrs McCann appears in the media urging people to pray for her daughter. As time goes on, they make public complaints about the lack of police cooperation. They also get a book publishing deal.

The investigation splits into two online factions – those who believe the McCanns are complicit in their daughter's disappearance, and those who believe it was an intruder. One theory is that the McCanns gave their child too much of an over-the-counter cough medicine to help her sleep.

She dies, and the parents, believing they will lose their jobs working in a hospital, decide to set up a fake abduction. Their relative wealth, discrepancies in accounts, and behaviour, are all seen as them being complicit.

The other side argue that being rich is not a crime, no one knows how they would react if they were put into a similar situation, and the police were simply not trained to deal with such a serious incident as a child abduction. It is possible an intruder came in through the damaged window and carried Madeleine away. Detectives from Scotland Yard were requested to help with the investigation. In 2013 they believed there were over forty people of interest, although it is not known if the McCanns were on the list. In 2015 the British Government disclosed that they had so far spent ten million pounds dealing with what is still listed as a missing persons enquiry, rather than an abduction or a murder. But in 2020 police revealed that a 43-year-old German prisoner has been identified as a suspect as he was in Portugal at the time of the disappearance. The McCanns thank police, saying: "All we have ever wanted is to find her, uncover the truth and bring those responsible to justice. We will never give up hope of finding Madeleine alive, but whatever the outcome may be, we need to know as we need to find peace." The German suspect has never confessed to abducting or killing Madeleine McCann. At the time of writing this book in 2023 enquiries are still ongoing.

This seems to be another investigation filled with "what if's". What if a witness had seen the intruder, what if the police hadn't messed up the crime scene, what if the parents are covering for each other, what if DNA technology finally catches the criminal? Like the Ramseys, the McCanns have been under constant scrutiny ever since they lost their daughter. It is also another crime that has taken hold of the public's interest, especially on the internet. To some extent each family now live in a virtual prison after being judged in the court of public opinion.

After JonBenét's death the Ramseys spent the next two years appearing on television when they should have been looking for their daughter's killer. You can argue that's the job of the police; but the Ramsey's continued to paint the police as incompetent. They did offer a reward for any information about the intruder, $50,000.00, less than half of what the kidnapper demanded. The clothing worn on Christmas night and the next day had still not been seized. The police kept requesting them, but it was nearly a year before John and Patsy finally handed over their clothes.

Detective Steve Thomas resigned from the police because of what he saw as more than just incompetence in the District Attorney's office. He believed that the

closeness between the D.A's office and the Ramsey
Defence Team had allowed someone to get away with
murder. Thomas' resignation came in the form of a letter he
sent to the newspapers. It was a damming indictment of
just how weak the justice system had become since the trial
of O.J. Simpson a few years before. The public demanded
answers. The Governor of Colorado stepped in. He
overruled Alex Hunter and insisted that a grand jury be
formed to look at the evidence and decide if there was
enough to charge anyone involved in the death of
JonBenét. If Hunter disagreed, he would be dismissed. And
so, in 1998 twelve people were sworn in by a court judge.
Alex Hunter demanded that the intruder theory be heard by
the jury, which was quite unusual as it was not part of the
police evidence package. Lou Smit, who was by now a
private detective working for the Ramseys, would be
allowed to give his theory on how the intruder would have
committed the crime. A handwriting expert working for the
Ramseys was also allowed to give evidence. Fleet White
and Linda Hoffman gave evidence, as well as Burke
Ramsey. The only two people who didn't give evidence
was John and Patsy. This is another strange aspect of the
trial, as they were still witnesses and could have given
evidence of that day. Their argument was that they had
only been interviewed a few months before and had

recently handed over the clothes they were wearing on Christmas night. There is also the argument that although they would have attended as witnesses, they could have been cross examined.

The jury took over a year to hear the evidence that was available at the time. As the records are still closed, we don't know what information they were given. We know the jury attended the house, paying particular attention to the wine cellar (with the light switched on and then off), and the basement window. After a week of deliberation, on October 13th, 1998, out of seven possible offences, they put forward two prosecution charges for both John and Patsy. That -

"On or between December 25, and December 26, 1996, in Boulder County, Colorado, John Ramsey/Patsy Ramsey did unlawfully, knowingly recklessly and feloniously permit a child to be unreasonably placed in a situation which posed a threat to the child's life or health, which resulted in the death of JonBenet Ramsey, a child under the age of sixteen."

"On or about December 25, and December 26, 1996 in Boulder County, Colorado, John Ramsey/Patsy Ramsey did unlawfully, knowingly, and feloniously render assistance to a person, with intent to hinder, delay and prevent the

discovery, detention, apprehension, prosecution, conviction and punishment of such person for the commission of a crime, knowing the person being assisted has committed and was suspected of the crime of murder in the first degree and child abuse resulting in death."

We should note that neither charge is in relation to murder. What is clear is that the jury believed both John and Patsy had knowledge of another's actions that night, and that both could be involved in some way of allowing the death of JonBenét. Both were believed to have either hindered the police investigation in some way, and/or knew that the other party had also tried to hinder the investigation. But perhaps the real sting in these charges was in the tail. The part where it states, *"knowing the person being assisted, has committed, and was suspected, of the crime of murder in the first degree and child abuse resulting in death."* It meant that if either John or Patsy had been convicted of hindering the investigation, their co-defendant could face a further charge of murder. An example would be if the jury believed that Patsy had written the ransom note, John could have been charged with child abuse; unless of course one of them was willing to make a plea bargain.

Some people have also said that the charges could relate to Burke being the person the parents' rendered assistance to. As the wording of the charges had been written out by a legal expert, who would have been aware that Burke was under the age of criminal responsibility at the time JonBenét died, the first charge might relate to this. Although we must remember John and Patsy had allowed Burke to give evidence (we just don't know what he said).

We must also remember a Grand Jury is used to see if there is enough to charge someone with an offence. All they need for this is probable cause. If they do, then another trial will be held, for which the burden of proof to secure a conviction must be beyond all reasonable doubt. If the jury do not formulate a charge, then the police investigation continues. This means that every member of the jury is bound by law not to reveal anything about what had gone on during those months when they heard the evidence.

That afternoon just two weeks before Halloween Alex Hunter stepped up to the podium to tell the waiting journalists and members of the public news about the American Justice System. "The grand jurors have done their work extremely well, bringing to bear all their legal powers, life experiences, and shrewdness. ... I must report to you that I and my prosecution task force believe we do not have sufficient evidence to warrant the filing of charges against anyone who has been investigated at this time.

Under no circumstances will I or any of my advisers, prosecutors, the law-enforcement officers working on this case, or the grand jurors discuss grand-jury proceedings, today or forever, unless ordered by the court."

Just like the ransom note, the key message was hidden between lines of deception. There would be no charges; but it seemed more important for Mr Hunter to remind the jury members they could face prosecution if they said anything to anyone. It's because he knew. He knew they had spent a year on the investigation and had come up with the decision to charge John and Patsy. Within the space of an hour, he had overturned it. As the District Attorney in charge of the investigation, he had that right. He might have been concerned that the Ramsey Defence Team would do what O.J. Simpson's team did: destroy the integrity of police procedures rather than prove their client's innocence. Hunter might have also been concerned that a trial would expose who had told police that morning to treat the Ramseys as victims, who had refused the police requests to arrest Patsy in those important first weeks, who had blocked numerous warrants, and who had been informing the press and the defence team about the investigation. Not only could a trial have resulted in no one being found guilty, it could have highlighted major issues within the justice system itself.

The Ramsey Defence Team declared John and Patsy as proven innocent. The public were denied the truth. Within a year John and Patsy published their first book, *The death of Innocence*. In it they said that the jury's decision not to indict them after hearing all the evidence was a vindication of their innocence. It was not until 2013 that the public were finally informed that the jury were willing to prosecute John and Patsy, but by then so much time had passed.

There was also a second court case involving the Ramseys, although this one did not gain as much publicity. In their book they had named Chris Woolf among a list of possible suspects. Wolf, a local journalist, was a suspect because an ex-girlfriend told police she did not know where he was on Christmas night. She also claimed that his writing looked like the ransom note, that he thought big corporations such as Access Graphics were immoral, he knew someone who worked for the company, and she was sure he once had a sweatshirt with SBTC on it. He took a handwriting test, and it was negative, the sweatshirt (Santa Barbara Tennis Club?) was never found. His DNA did not match any found at the crime scene. Wolf said he was asleep on Christmas night (as did Patsy). He did have a degree in journalism (as did Patsy) and he did know someone who worked for Access Graphics (as did Pasty). Wolf felt that the act of naming him was malicious and defamatory, so he sued the Ramsey's for fifty million dollars. But instead of trying to clear his name, he did nothing apart from get an expert to say he didn't write the ransom note. Strangely, although this was an ideal moment to see if Chris Wolf had killed their child, the Ramseys spent all their time in court pointing out that an intruder (no matter who it was) had committed the crime.

This allowed the Ramseys to claim the intruder theory as fact when it clearly wasn't. The words in Italics are what the Ramsey Defence Team put forward as evidence. *The knot and the garotte was all part of a sophisticated bondage device that could only have been done by an (adult) intruder.* There is no proof of this. *A fibre of animal hair belonging to a beaver was found on the duct tape, and the Ramseys claimed not to own any item of clothing that contained beaver fur.* The district attorney had refused to give the police warrants to search for items of clothing; as such the Ramseys only gave the police what they wanted to give. *The shoeprints in the basement were recently made.* There is no proof that the shoeprints had been made the same time as JonBenét being put in the wine cellar. In such a sterile environment they could have been made weeks or even months before. *The jury were told that no one in the house owned H-Tech boots.* This was also untrue, as Burke owned a pair, but that information was not in the public domain at the time. *There was an unidentified palm print on the wine cellar door.* The print had been identified as belonging to John's oldest daughter. As she had not been to the address in months, it also helps prove that a shoe print could also have been there for months. *A baseball bat that the Ramseys could not recall owning was found outside with fibres from the basement carpet on it.* In 2016 Burke finally stated it was his baseball bat. *The autopsy report showed JonBenét was conscious when being strangled and fought her attacker.* The autopsy report showed no such thing. *There was unidentified male DNA under her fingernails.* The DNA was of such low quality that it could have been there for days, if not weeks. And none of it was ever classified as skin tissue, meaning she didn't get it fighting off her attacker. *The autopsy report says that the head injury happened at the same time as the strangulation.* It doesn't. At the grand jury trial one of the best head trauma experts in America concluded that the skull fracture was caused between 45 minutes to 2 hours before she died. They also informed the grand jury that JonBenét would also have shown signs of Brain Damage, ie, unconscious, vital organs shutting down. This also contradicts the theory that she struggled while being strangled. None of this was said in the civil trial. *There was male DNA found under a right fingernail, male DNA found under a left fingernail, and male DNA found on the underwear and long-johns, which does not match that of any of the Ramseys.* This seems to imply that all the DNA comes from the same unknown male. It did not. The quality of the DNA is so weak that the best we can say is that the DNA could have come from about a hundred and fifty million people living in America, and if you firmly believe the DNA was linked to the intruder theory you would also have to say that there were possibly three suspects who entered the house than night.

The only DNA that would be able to be tested and compared on the national database was the one found on the underwear. It is believed to be half a nanogram of unknown male DNA. Touching an item anytime between fifteen to thirty seconds will leave about two hundred nanograms of DNA. The only people who believed that an intruder left that DNA was the Ramsey Defence Team. *A stun gun was used on the six-year-old child, and the Ramseys do not own one.* There has never been any scientific proof that a stun gun was used. *The Ramseys always helped police with their enquiries.* They refused numerous requests. *The end of the paintbrush and the origins of the duct tape and white cord where never found, meaning someone must have left with them.* You could also argue that the Ramseys were never searched when they left that day and could have walked out of the house carrying anything. *There had been numerous parties before Christmas, to which several people could have learnt the layout of the house.* They would also need to know that the alarm would not be turned on, the dog would be with a neighbour, the basement window would not be locked, the basement door would not be locked, there would be no guests staying the night, and that the family would be asleep by 10.30pm.

In fact, neither Chris Wolf nor the Ramseys seemed to understand what the trial was there for. Wolf never really prosecuted the Ramseys for deformation, and the Ramseys never really proved that Wolf was a viable suspect. You could wonder why the civil trial took place at all. When O.J. Simpson was found not guilty in a criminal trial, under the double jeopardy rules at the time could not be accused of the same crime again. Soon after being released, he was accused in relation to a civil matter, not for murder, but wrongful death. On the balance of probabilities, he was found guilty. Some people may argue that the Chris Woolf civil case, coming straight off the back of the Grand Jury investigation, was set up to make sure the Ramseys could never be prosecuted in a civil case if they were also found not guilty in a criminal trial. More importantly, the theory of an intruder killing JonBenét was now classed as more probable than one of the Ramseys doing it.

Chapter 25

Ten Questions.

Dying is a very simple thing. I've looked at death and really, I know. If I should have died it would have been very easy for me. Quite the easiest thing I ever did. But the people at home do not realize that. They suffer a thousand times more.

Ernest Hemingway.

Even after all these years this is still a live investigation. Some information has never been disclosed to the public. So, we will give ourselves ten questions to try and resolve the issue of whether it was an intruder or a member of the family who were involved.

1. What time did they leave Fleet White's house? Or to be more precise, what time did they get home? The police have never been able to release part of Fleet White's statement in relation to when the Ramsey's left on Christmas night. Nor have they ever released statements from the two families

that the Ramseys dropped gifts for that night to say if they saw JonBenét alive or asleep? The answer of what time the Ramseys got home would help to clear that argument about John and Patsy lying to the police.

2. Why was the ransom note written?

We can argue who may have written it, but we should also ask why. Is it really a ransom note, or a story to cover up something else. If it's true, why is it so long, why didn't they ask for more money, and more importantly, why did they take the (dead or alive) body with them? If the ransom note is false, then making it so long can only be because the writer wanted whoever was reading it to believe this was real kidnapping. The flaw is that the writer failed to see that they had overreached themselves. We can only say that if the ransom note had not been written the police would have arrested John and Patsy.

3. What was the time of death?

I don't know why any medical professional did not give an estimated time of death. Witnesses all say JonBenét was in full rigor mortis when she was found at 1pm. So, let's say she died between 10.30pm of the 25th and 1am of the 26th December. If we put the head injury happening ninety minutes before JonBenét died, we are in the realms of when the Ramseys originally said they got home. If the Ramseys were truly innocent they would want to know the time of death, if only because they put on JonBenét's gravestone that she died on the 25th of December.

4. Food for Thought.

Time of death also factors in the bowl of pineapple. If you believe it's not really pineapple in her stomach, that's fine, but the bowl of pineapple in the breakfast room is real, so are Burke and Patsy's fingerprints are. The bowl could have been put out at any time on Christmas day, but no one seems to know anything about it. The best Patsy could do is say she would not have got such a large spoon to use. This is not good enough. You got the bowl out, or you did not. Why no one can account for the bowl is because JonBenét must have eaten sometime between 10 and 11.30pm, which is the opposite of her falling asleep in the car and being carried up to her bedroom.

5. Clothing.

    There is one photograph of JonBenét taken on
    Christmas morning wearing pink pyjamas. These
    must have been the ones put under her pillow. In
    her first account Patsy tells police the red turtleneck
    top crumbled up in the bathroom is what JonBenét
    went to bed wearing. It is difficult to see how the
    wife of a multi-millionaire would let her daughter
    go to sleep on Christmas night in a pair of used
    boys long johns. Patsy said in a later interview the
    size 12 underwear the six-year-old JonBenét was
    wearing when she was found in the basement was
    part of a pack of seven and meant to be a Christmas
    gift to John's daughter. Presumably they were not
    among the presents that John took to the airport on
    Christmas day, or the presents found partially
    opened in the wine cellar. So how did they end up
    on JonBenét, and where are the other six pairs? I
    would also ask that if this was a Christmas present
    for John's other daughter to open in Michigan, how
    did JonBenét know about them?

    On the same theme, it is also not clear where the
    boys' long johns came from. They are described as
    "well used" and slightly too small for JonBenét.
    This seems strange when you consider they were

put on while she was lying asleep in her own bedroom. It is unlikely they were in JonBenét's wardrobe, and if they were piled among the other twenty bed-time clothes in the drawer in the bathroom, surely, there were better options? But then, Patsy makes no mention of going into the bathroom to select the long johns, so on what night before Christmas did JonBenét wear them and leave them near the bed? It's possible that they were Burke's from a few years ago. It's also possible that they belonged to another boy. There is a bin bag of old clothing by the spiral staircase that the family were going to give to charity. They could have come from there. But If Patsy did not put them on her daughter while she was asleep in her bed, who did?

There is the pink Barbie nightgown found next to JonBenét in the wine cellar. How did this get spots of blood on it? Was the blood fresh, did it look as if it had dripped onto the top, were they splash marks, or had they soaked through from an abrasion? Were the traces of urine visible, an if Burke's and Patsy's DNA were found on the nightgown, when did JonBenét last wear the top. We know it wasn't Christmas eve.

6. Marks on the body

You could argue that a kidnapper has no reason to cause the minor injuries found on JonBenet's body. They make no difference to the end result apart from the kidnapper spending more time in the home. The marks on the neck would not have silenced her more effectively than simply placing a hand (or duct tape) over her mouth. The two sets of marks on the face and back make no sense if she was conscious. Evidence of trauma in the vagina also shows it was washed afterwards. But there is also the issue that she has urinated while lying face down. I don't know if she was washed down and then turned over, and then carried into the wine cellar; or, she has urinated, the long-johns removed, she is washed down, and the wet Long-johns put back on. Either way, time is still moving on.

It also leads to the conclusion that this was not a rush attack where all the injuries were carried out in a matter of minutes. If you factor in the head injury there is at least an hour when the person involved was in the home. The tying of the wrists and using cord and a broken paintbrush to form a garotte must have also taken time. The intruder theory and this being a brutal attack is difficult to maintain when we know that after her death someone seems to have taken care of JonBenét. If she died face down on the carpeted area of the boiler room, someone has then moved her into the wine cellar with the concrete floor, but they have wrapped her in a white blanket as if they didn't want her to be injured any further.

7. There's a ghost in my house.

Were there any signs in the house that showed someone had been wearing gloves? An intruder would not bother cleaning away anything they touched if they had been, but they would undoubtedly leave smudge marks. The best place for this would be the window in the basement. Someone climbing through it for the first time would remove the shards of glass still in the frame. They may also go in backwards to try to ease themselves down. Either way, they will be moving their hands around trying to judge (in the dark) how far down they will have to jump. And if someone had to use a suitcase to help get out, they would presumably have placed both gloved hands on the frame and the windowsill and lifted themselves until they could get at least one knee on the windowsill.

We also have the paintbrush. No one seems to have touched the part used on the garotte and the piece placed back in the paint tray. And what about the piece of duct tape. If you are wearing gloves, whether latex or leather, they would leave a trace. Did forensic officers find any glove marks in the bedroom or the basement. We should also ask the question, did anywhere show signs of having been recently cleaned? The lack of forensic evidence in relation to an intruder points to a clever criminal. The lack of evidence on the people who live in the house points to a cover-up.

8. Wake up call.

What happened between 5.30 and 6am? John gets up with his alarm. Patsy says she gets up while John is in the shower. She goes to the bathroom, brushes her teeth, gets dressed in the clothes she wore the night before and puts on her make-up. John is still in the shower. She walks across the other side of the house to use the back stairs, checks JonBenét's bedroom (in some accounts), then washes an item of clothing belonging to JonBenét.

John is still in the shower. Patsy goes down the spiral staircase, reaches the bottom, reads a bit of the ransom note, goes back upstairs, realises JonBenét is not in her bedroom, and calls out for John. He comes down just in a pair of boxer shorts. They possibly both go across the whole of the house to check on Burke, then come all the way back across the house and go down the spiral staircase. John presumably takes the pieces of paper, puts them on the floor (for some reason he is unable to stand and read at the same time). He reads the note (from start to finish?). Patsy asks if they should call the police. John must be on the second page by now, because he would later say that even though the kidnapper's told him not to, he tells Patsy to call police.

5.52am. Patsy makes the call. She speaks to the police controller for less than two minutes. She then hangs up. There is then possibly the sound of Patsy and another person speaking in the background. Patsy then calls two friends. She must tell them what has happened and asks them to come over. Meanwhile, John has gone back up two flights of stairs to get dressed. He is downstairs fully dressed four minutes later when police come to the door.

They take police through the house and show officer French the Ransom note that is still on the floor near the spiral staircase (why didn't Patsy read it?). John mentions that he has searched for any open doors or windows (when/whereabout in the house?). Officer French does not notice the flashlight in the kitchen, even though its still dark.

The Ramseys tell police that the alarm was not set last night, and that none of the windows appear damaged (who checked?). Police are also told at least six people have a front door key, including the housekeeper. They are told that Burke is safe and well in his bedroom. It's possible that John had spent twenty minutes in the shower that morning, and Patsy sat and did nothing after the phone calls, but why didn't John check the house with officer French, and why didn't Patsy read the ransom note?

9. Where is the missing evidence?
   If we look at the intruder theory, we know that the kidnapper did not have a ransom note when they broke in. We must assume they had (possibly gloves) duct tape, cord, a blade to cut the cord, an object to hit JonBenét on the head with, perhaps a stun gun, and possibly even a flashlight. If not, they

were extremely lucky that this one house contained all the items they needed, and that they managed to find them in the dark. Someone taking these items when they left certainly explains why the items were never found. But how else could they have been disposed?

Police footage shows the part of the basement where Patsy made her decorations. There are scissors, boxes, different types of ribbons and tape. Going past the laundry area the camera points towards the other storage room. Just to the right of the frame is what appears to be a large steel manhole cover/storm drain key. It makes me wonder if under the carpet somewhere there is a drain. Older houses had basements which may have been dug deeper than the drains running along the street. We know there is a restroom in the basement, plus a washing machine. Both would need separate drains to wash the water away. You could also use them to wash away bits of cord, the tip of a paintbrush and duct tape. In fact, apart from the flashlight not only did the intruder find everything they wanted, but they also found everything that could float.

10. Is this the real life, is this just fantasy?

With true crime we can often compare one case to another. We do it to look for patterns, to highlight the way justice works, and no doubt we can assure ourselves that on the balance of probabilities the crime/investigation happened the way the book/documentary/podcast said it happened. True crime also grounds us in reality. Real people were involved. But with this investigation I kept going back to works of fiction. *Murder on the Orient Express, Zodiac, Anatomy of a Murder, Rashomon, Séance on a wet Afternoon*, 12 Angry Men, to name a few. The only reason I can think of is that the death of JonBenét Ramsey has two narratives running all the way through it. The first includes the police and District Attorney's Office, and the people whose lives have all been affected by this tragedy. But there has always been another story which runs like a work of fiction. The problem with this second narrative is that it feels as though there are scenes or pages missing, or things that don't make sense.

If we continue with one narrative being fictions, in *To Kill a Mockingbird*, Atticus Finch tells his daughter, "The one thing that does not abide by majority rule is a person's conscience." If we were to bring in our list of suspects and ask them the single question: Why did she have to die? What would the answer be? An intruder would have the greatest difficulty in claiming it was an accident. They have broken in with the intent to commit one crime. Whatever happened next, they should not have been there in the first place. If you spoke to someone who lived in the house, how could they explain the garotte? The evidence shows that JonBenét was still breathing when the cord was put around her neck. She may not have been conscious, she may have even been brain dead, but it was not up to that person to play God on Christmas night.

Perhaps the question should not be about death, but life. A six-year-old girl might not know what it means to be alive, but they know what it means to be happy or sad. Their hopes and fears would come and go like musical notes. For them the universe extends no further than home, family, friends, and school. Time consists of bed, food, playing, and back to bed. Adults can claim to be wiser, but that does not make them happier. Adults know there are places we must go even when we may not want to. There is time spent on things we can't get out of, memories we can never erase. Adults understand that being alive is more than just the body, it is a state of mind. Some reach an age where they say they would rather get cancer and know they are going to die than a degenerative brain disease and end up not having clue what their name is. They might also say that if it ever got to that stage, they would want someone to end their silent suffering. And if you had a loved one in that situation, what would you do? Would you continue to care for them even though the person you knew had gone? Or if you believe that their spirit was now Heaven, would you sign the hospitals *Do Not Resuscitate* form? And what if you had to make that choice in the basement of your home?

Chapter 26

The Court of Public Opinion.

There are those in our own country too who today speak of the 'protection of country,' of 'survival'. A decision must be made in the life of every nation at the very moment when the grasp of the enemy is at its throat. Then, it seems that the only way to survive is to use the means of the enemy, to rest survival upon what is expedient, to look the other way. Well, the answer to that is 'survival as what'? A country isn't a rock. It's not an extension of oneself. It's what it stands for. It's what it stands for when standing for something is the most difficult! Before the people of the world, let it now be noted that here, in our decision, this is what we stand for: Justice, truth, and the value of a single human being.

Judgement at Nuremburg. Directed by Stanley Kramer, 1959.

What if the District Attorney had agreed with the Grand Jury and charged John and Patsy. Just like O.J. Simpson, the Ramsey's would have got a good lawyer. When I say *good,* I mean lawyers such as Johnnie Cochran and Carl Douglas, who were considered by some to have no morals or integrity, but they knew how a trial worked. This is not to discredit men such as this. We can all dream about going to court believing in justice with a lawyer such as Atticus Finch, but he lost his case.

And the Ramsey's had the assumption of innocence on their side when it came to DNA or fibre evidence. Anything linked to the defendants could be because they lived in the same house. Any arguments about there being no evidence of an intruder entering the house that night can be answered by the failure of the police to secure the scene. But let's go through each defendant in our imaginary trial: John.

"On or between December 25, and December 26, 1996, in Boulder County, Colorado, John Ramsey did unlawfully, knowingly recklessly and feloniously permit a child to be unreasonably placed in a situation which posed a threat to the child's life or health, which resulted in the death of JonBenet Ramsey, a child under the age of sixteen."

This could be in relation to when JonBenét is in the basement and the garotte is put around her neck. The difficulty any prosecution would have in putting this case to a jury is that John was one of the last people to see JonBenét alive, and the first person to find her. Forensic evidence does not prove his guilt. The issue of any prior sexual abuse is not conclusive. There is nothing in his behaviour on Christmas night and the next day that can be argued as a submission of guilt.

Any cross examination would find it difficult to prove he committed the offences he had been charged with. John has Patsy as a witness for when he put JonBenét on her bed. He goes to bed, although it's strange that they don't go to bed at the same time, say nothing to each other while in their bed on Christmas night, and do not witness each other getting out of bed in the morning. He was ruled out as the writer of the ransom note. He is the one who tells Patsy to call the police. In relation to the basement window and suitcase he eventually tells police. There is also a witness to when he enters the wine cellar. That leaves the prosecution trying to convince the jury the forensic evidence proves this case.

As a jury member I would first be asking what type of DNA we are talking about. Most people would expect the DNA found under the fingernail to be skin cells where JonBenét scratched the offender, but it isn't. As for the DNA on the clothing and the underwear, if it was found on the front of her body, could it have come from the carpet when she was lying down. I would also be asking if there was any DNA belonging to John that had been found somewhere that cannot be explained. The answer appears to be No.

The same can also be said about any clothing fibres linked to John. At least John changed his clothes the next morning, but again, it seems strange that it took a year for John and Patsy to hand over the clothes they wore on Christmas night; surely Johns clothes were left in the bedroom? In the end we simply have a long list of circumstantial evidence which needs to be weighed and measured against John's defence – that an intruder killed his daughter.

And John's defence team at part of this trial would focus on police procedure, and its subsequent failings. During the O.J. Simpson trial the defence team accused detective Mark Fuhrman of being racist, then used his silence to question every piece of evidence and police rationale. It would have been the same with the Ramsey Defence Team. They would have accused detective Linda Arndt of being incapable of dealing with the investigation, then made her a scapegoat for all police mistakes, especially the comments she made a few years after the event about counting the bullets in her gun

As this is a (theoretical) trial, the Ramsey Defence Team can also go for broke. They can say the reason no stranger has ever been caught is because the police stopped looking for one on the 26th of December 1996. That the flashlight belonged to the intruder, that a stun gun was used on JonBenét, the duct tape and white cord were taken away by the intruder. That this was a brutal attack by a sexual pervert with mental health issues who sexually assaulted JonBenét with the tip of the paintbrush and then kept it as a macabre souvenir. And any chance of gathering evidence was lost due to police failings. For every expert the prosecution brings out, the Ramsey Defence Team can bring out a better paid one. Remember, defence experts don't have to refute another expert's opinion, they just have to tell the jury that it may not be totally accurate.

The only change we can make to our make-believe trial is that we could consider evidence that may not have been deemed relevant at the Grand Jury hearing in 1999. It is believed that files were deleted from John Ramseys computer at some point before it was seized on the 26th December, but no one seemed to recognise its significance at the time. The police put in a warrant to examine all incoming and outgoing phone calls on the Ramseys phone. It was refused. It would be interesting to know if the phone line was connected to the internet on the old dialling system at a time when everyone was meant to be asleep. It would also be interesting to know if in 1996 a computer could be examined for its search history, especially in relation to *Kidnap Threats*. That doesn't mean John was using the computer that night anymore than it means he knew who wrote the ransom note.

Patsy.

For Patsy the second charged seems more appropriate:

"On or about December 25, and December 26, 1996 in Boulder County, Colorado, Patsy Ramsey did unlawfully, knowingly, and feloniously render assistance to a person, with intent to hinder, delay and prevent the discovery, detention, apprehension, prosecution, conviction and punishment of such person for the commission of a crime, knowing the person being assisted has committed and was suspected of the crime of murder in the first degree and child abuse resulting in death."

This seems to be in relation to the ransom note.

We already have an issue in that Patsy's handwriting experts have said she didn't fully match all the characteristics to prove she wrote the note (although even the experts she paid for were unable to totally rule her out). But the ransom note comes down to one simple fact: whoever wrote it was also involved in the death of JonBenét. If I was a member of the jury, I would ask the question: Is everything in the ransom note true, and if not, which parts are a lie? This may seem strange, but if this was a real kidnapping, the writer may lie about being a small foreign faction, but they would still want John to believe they have his child. They want money. They want him to do what they say. So, if you believe it was an intruder you must believe they are telling the truth in at least ninety percent of this ransom note. The only issue is that the possible lies seem to downplay the kidnappers role rather than exaggerate them. Why not describe yourself as a large foreign faction, why not demand a million dollars, and tell John that a group of twelve angry men are watching his daughter.

You could argue that the "small foreign faction" is a lie to make the police look away from people who knew about John's business life. But if it was someone linked to the company, would they really demand John's Christmas bonus of 118k. Wouldn't that make the police more likely to investigate everyone connected with Access Graphics? There is also the factor of the time it took to write the note. Why write out a lie when it makes no difference to the aim of the kidnapper. So, either everything in the ransom note, including the two men watching over his daughter, is true; or someone has spent over thirty minutes writing a piece of total fiction.

We know the writer of the note has tried to hide their writing style. We also know Patsy had a copy of the ransom note when asked to give a handwriting sample and she could have done her utmost to change her style, but she was still linked to it. The usual reply is that there was only a partial match. But if you add to this the chances of a kidnapper having a similar writing style to Patsy and the odds are a couple of million to one. The Ramsey Defence Team have tried to argue that someone could have broken in and spent a few hours copying Patsy's style to deflect attention away from themselves, but if even Patsy couldn't differentiate between her own handwriting and the person who wrote the ransom note, the writer must have taken years to get it that perfect.

We have not even gone through the fibres from Patsy's clothes found under the duct tape. Transference, claim the defence. OK, but what about her clothing fibres found inside the knot of new white cord used for the garotte, how could they have got there when at no point has Patsy gone near JonBenet's head when she was carried out of the car and into her bed. You also have the links between Patsy and the fact it was her paintbrush that was used, her notepad, the note left on the spiral staircase that she always uses, and her fingerprints on the bowl of pineapple.

The changes in her accounts could be considered circumstantial. As would any account from Linda Hoffman. She was to tell police that she believed Patsy had multiple personalities and had seen her punish JonBenét for wetting the bed on previous occasions. But the Ramsey Defence Team could argue that Linda Hoffman had a grudge after being named as a possible suspect by the Ramseys. Interestingly, this "Grudge" against the Ramseys could be used by everyone who had been suspected by the Ramseys and were called to give evidence in our fictional trial. Even Fleet White, whose testimony would be vital, could be accused of trying to implicate the Ramseys ever since he was named as a suspect by them. In the end, after all the forensic evidence and witness testimonies had been examined and cross examined, it feels as though it still comes down to the ransom note. I cant think of a line more excruciating than "If the glove don't fit, you must acquit", when dealing with a murder trial, but I think this imaginary jury would find themselves in the same situation as Simpson's jury.

Would any of them really believe that an intruder has managed to get into the house, write a ransom note, wait a few hours until the family returned home, keep hiding until everyone had gone to bed, get JonBenét up, feed her, spend time with her, assault her, strangle her, fracture her skull, and then escape without leaving any clues whatsoever? I would say No.

So, is there enough to prove beyond all reasonable doubt that John put his daughter in a situation that resulted in her death…I would also say No. We cannot say he is guilty when the evidence does not conclusively lead to him. We may not believe an intruder was involved, but circumstantial theories should never be enough to sentence someone to the death penalty.

The evidence against Patsy is a far clearer picture. I think the sheer number of her clothing fibres found on numerous items compared to the lack of fibres from an unknown person indicate that Patsy spent more time with JonBenét that night than any intruder. But Patsy is not on trial for murder. We need to prove beyond all reasonable doubt that she hindered the police investigation…and I think she would have been found guilty. If the police controller had finally been called to give evidence, her account of that morning, and her concerns that something was wrong, are damaging as Patsy has no defence for them. But the key factor is the ransom note. It only fits into the investigation if we treat it as a work of fiction, and the only reason someone would write it would be to cover up one crime with a different one. And as such, Patsy may not have killed her daughter, but she wrote the note.

As for what punishment she should receive I would like to think that there would be an element of mercy. Something happened in the house that night which led to a mother having to write the ransom note rather than seek medical help for her daughter. In crime fiction we would like a full confession, perhaps where Patsy admits to writing the ransom note but can honestly say the death of JonBenét was not deliberate. But the reality is the investigation never got this far, and it never will. Patsy Ramsey succumbed to cancer again and passed away in 2006. Her deathbed confession was that she was looking forward to seeing JonBenét again in Heaven. I hope she did.

Ransom Note	Patsy Ramsey
ʄ	ʄ
ʄ	ʄ
ʃ	ɡ
ɔ	ɔ
h	h
h	h
h	h

Chapter 27
Aftermath.

The pause makes you think the song will end. And then the song isn't really over, so you're relieved. But then the song does actually end, because every song ends, obviously, and THAT. TIME. THE. END. IS. FOR. REAL.

Jennifer Egan, *A Visit from the Goon Squad.*

Instead of a trial we were left to continue looking for answers somewhere within those two different stories running side by side. On January 1st, 1997, just a day after their daughter's funeral John and Patsy granted an interview to CNN. At the end Patsy proclaims, "There is a killer on the loose." The police carried out a press conference the next day to state that there was no lone killer stalking the streets of Colorado. The media quickly realised there was more going on her that a kidnapping/murder investigation. This heaped more pressure on the police, and to be fair, onto the Ramseys themselves. The silent conflict from both sides continued until August 1998 when Steve Thomas resigned as a detective. He publicly sends out an 8-page notice in which he calls Alex Hunter's D.A. office "thoroughly compromised". Here is part of his letter –

"During the investigation detectives would discover, collect, and bring evidence to the district attorney's office, only to have it summarily dismissed or rationalized as insignificant. The most elementary of investigative efforts, such as obtaining telephone and credit card records, were met without support, search warrants denied. The significant opinions of national experts were casually dismissed or ignored by the district attorney's office, even the experienced FBI were waved aside. Those who chose not to cooperate were never compelled before a grand jury early in this case, as detectives suggested only weeks after the murder, while information and memories were fresh.

In a departure from protocol, police reports, physical evidence, and investigative information we shared with Ramsey defense attorneys, all of this in the district attorney's office "spirit of cooperation". I served a search warrant, only to find later defense attorneys were simply given copies of the evidence it yielded. I was repeatedly reminded by some in the district attorney's office just how powerful and talented and resourceful particular defense attorneys were. How could decisions be made this way? Regretfully, I tender this letter, and my police career, a calling which I loved. I do this because I cannot continue to sanction by my silence what has occurred in this case. It was never a fair playing field, the "game" was simply unacceptable anymore. And that's what makes this all so painful. The detectives never had a chance. If ever there were a case, and if ever there were a victim, who truly meant something to the detectives pursuing the truth, this is it. If not this case, what case? Until such time an independent prosecutor is appointed to oversee this case, I will not be a part of this. What went on was simply wrong. I recalled a favorite passage recently, Atticus Finch speaking to his daughter: "Just remember that one thing does not abide by majority rule, Scout — it's your conscience."

The letter was enough for the governor of Colorado to get involved and tell the DA to get a Grand Jury hearing or resign. For some strange reason the D.A. did not subpoena John or Patsy but did allow Lou smit to give a lengthy presentation on the intruder theory, which was highly unusual. After the jury had spent a year hearing the evidence, they decided to indict John and Patsy Ramsey. Alex Hunter then made the judgement not to. He stated publicly that there was not sufficient evidence to file charges, making it sound as if John and Patsy were innocent. Why he did so, has never been fully resolved. By now Lou Smit had also resigned from the investigation. He worked solely for the Ramseys for the next couple of years trying to find an intruder that fitted all the pieces.

In 1999 came the first book about the death of JonBenét, *Perfect Murder, Perfect Town*, by Lawrence Schiller. It was an objective account from numerous sources. It was later turned into a TV film of the same name. Around the same time Linda Arndt also resigned from Boulder police, saying that those higher up in the justice system had let her take a lot of the blame for what happened that day. A few months later she gave an interview on television. She told the interviewer she believes she knows who killed JonBenét but refused to say their name for fear of being sued.

John and Patsy published their own book. They named an obscure person as a suspect and were taken to civil court for libel. The trial gave them a chance to again outline how an intruder could have carried out the killing. It also meant that their version of events became a matter of public record, making it almost impossible for anyone to take them to civil court for the death of their daughter. This wave carried them through the next couple of years where they would continue to go on television and say it must have been an intruder because of the unknown DNA.

The small foreign faction came back to bite America on September 11th 2001. The destruction of the Twin Towers, and the biggest assault on American soil since Pearl Harbour, showed that the country was not invincible. No matter how much money and power it had, it could not protect itself from the fact that political fundamentalism was being replaced by religious ones. Even the largest stray dog could not protect itself from a flea willing to die for a cause. Cells interlinked with cells.

In June 2006 Patsy Ramsey passed away from ovarian cancer. A few months later Mark Karr was deemed to be a credible suspect for police to arrest him in Thailand and bring him back for questioning. Their suspicions were based on Karr telling someone online that he accidentally killed JonBenét while making love to her. Within ten minutes of being interviewed it is clear he did not do it. In 2008 the new District Attorney Mary Lacy delivered a letter by hand to John Ramsey formally clearing him, Burke, and Patsy, from the investigation. Her reasons for doing so were that DNA on the waistband of the long-johns JonBenét was wearing matched the DNA left in her underwear. Many forensic experts and those in the legal profession were shocked at this exoneration. The DNA on both items did not prove it was an intruder. In fact, Mary Lacy knew that the DNA on JonBenét and the clothes showed traces of more than one person, too small to get a full profile, possibly because they had deteriorated by being on the clothes for weeks or even months, and none of them good enough to be able to compare on the DNA database. The current count lists six different DNA profiles, none of them good enough to be able to obtain a result. There was nothing to suggest John or Patsy should have been completely ruled out of the investigation, but it ended any chance of anyone from that house going to court. It would now be almost impossible to indict John unless compelling new evidence was found. Lou Smit continued to find his ghostly intruder without luck until he passed away in 2010. His family have continued his quest, but after nearly thirty years they have still not had a result.

By now Barack Obama was President. Many Americans must have felt that racism was finally over. In the new spirit of hope and justice, Obama created the Presidential Commission. Originally set up to look into police practices and any miscarriages of justice, it quickly became a platform for racial politics. If you were a white victim of crime, you would receive no outside help into your police investigation. The clock was now ticking as to when there would be no one left trying to find out who killed JonBenét Ramsey.

Other books were published. Not only by Steve Thomas and the Ramsey's but also by another detective involved in the case, James Kolar. In 2012 he published *Foreign Faction, who really kidnapped JonBenét?* This book put Burke as being the instigator of events that night. There is a further shock in 2013 when it is finally revealed the Grand Jury wanted to indict John and Patsy Ramsey on two counts each of child abuse resulting in their daughter's death.

In 2016, twenty years after the death of JonBenét, Boulder police confirm they have so far processed over 1,500 pieces of evidence, taken 200 DNA samples, interviewed more than 1,000 people in eight states, and investigated more than 20,000 tips, letters and e-mails to try and put closure on this case. This same year Burke gives his first televised interview. There are a few revelations. He thinks the flashlight might belong to the family, and the black baseball bat was his. For some of the questions Burke cannot recall as it was so long ago. It transpires the interview is in defence of a new documentary series on the killing of JonBenét which heavily implies that Burke killed his sister. The documentary series was drastically cut, the television company was sued for millions of dollars. How much they paid out is not known. The documentary eventually ended up on Youtube.

It appears there was too much news in 2016. Bill Cosby, the man who rose to fame in the nineties as America's father, stood accused on numerous counts of sexual assaults on young women. Another American who made millions in the nineties was also making the headlines. Donald Trump was about to become the next president. His main rival Hilary Clinton, wife of ex-president Bill, was caught out by numerous emails which showed her to be just as duplicitous as her husband. Luckily, she was not impeached. Those watching footage of the JonBenét investigation in 1996 must have wondered what the hell had happened to America in the last twenty years.

There were other tv documentaries about the case, and other books. But it soon became clear that some people were being paid by the Ramseys to promote the intruder theory as a way of it being fact rather than opinion. So, many people turned to the virtual world. Youtube sites such as *True Crime Rocket Science*, *Carmen Sandiego*, *True Crime Oracle*, *The Ramsey Case,* all covered the investigation in far more detail. The internet had podcasts talking about the investigation, with people believing that there was more honesty in *The Joe Rogan Show* than what they found on the mainstream media.

We still have the two narratives running side by side. Sometimes one takes the lead, then the other theory becomes the official version of events. The Ramsey Defence Team is still willing to publicly talk about a DNA breakthrough, possibly because it's never going to give a result. They claim the world is waiting for those tiny fragments of DNA to finally reveal the truth. But what truth? We already know the DNA belongs to a male, but even a better profile still relies on someone linked to the same genetic ancestry to be on the database. And if that male is found, what if he was a boy at the time, what if he has a rock-solid alibi. Do we treat a different tiny particle of DNA as belonging to the intruder. What is the future of this investigation?

There were those who thought the term of Trump could not get any worse, and then Joe Biden became President. We seem to have gone full circle putting people of power into positions that they are not able to make decisions in. How America got from Roosevelt to Kennedy to Biden in John Ramsey's lifetime is testimony to how far the country has fallen. In a far shorter space, the fact that truth, justice, and the American way has fallen out of favour with the children who are JonBenét's age had she had lived, makes me wonder if her death will ever be solved.

Chapter 28

And in the end the love you take
is equal to the love you make.

I would rather not go

Back to the old house

There's too many

Bad memories

Too many memories

There.

　　The Smiths, *Back to the Old House.*

They say that if you stare into to the microscope for too
long you will eventually find monsters. Throughout the
twentieth century America was undoubtably the greatest
country in the world. It saved us all from destruction. It
showed us how far we could go with democracy and free
speech. But by 1996 the seeds of America's demise were
already being sown. The country that had fought a civil war
to abolish slavery found that the battle wasn't over. The
belief in Justice was being eroded by the very people meant
to be protecting in. Now that people were going out with

video cameras and filming what they saw happening on the streets, those sitting at home were wondering who the guilty really were? We had lost faith in God, and now we were beginning to lose faith in ourselves.

The millennium saw the end of national identity and the birth of a genetic one. DNA became more important than USA. People stopped looking up to the flag and started spending all their time looking down into a screen. Race, gender, and sexuality took precedence over religion, government, and society as the voice of the individual became more important than the concerns of the community. As we stared ever deeper into the virtual world we began to lose sight of reality. We have online friends but never speak to our neighbour's. We talk about historic racism and while keeping quiet about where our phones and clothes come from. Men can be women as everyone demands freedom of speech and equality; but no one can ever question positive discrimination. Saving the planet is important, but no one is going to tell China to stop using coal. We literally have every book ever written at out fingertips, but instead we play Candy Crush. It may sound a bit like Joey B Toonz video, but it's important to remember we can't look at the JonBenét case without looking at how much society has changed.

Today there is a clamour to demand that every item from the JonBenét Ramsey case to be tested for DNA with no understanding of how or why, and what they expect the results to give them. But it's a good soundbite. It makes the news. Her face still sells. In the nineties we were shocked at the provocative footage of JonBenét in beauty pageants, but stores are selling lipsticks and boob tubes to six-year-old girls today. We believed in 1996 that those same images of JonBenét could have been the motivation for a sexual predator; but today a nine-year-old boy with a mobile phone has access to more hardcore porn in an hour than what most men would see in a year back then. The O.J. Simpson trial is seen as a low point in race relations, but if you blame Simpson's acquittal on racial politics, where does that put the white community for the failure to charge anyone with JonBenét's death? Perhaps the great American tragedy is that we have lost the ability to judge what is right or wrong because our old values do not make sense anymore. So, out of all the other hundreds of child murders that have occurred in the last twenty years, why does this one still seems so important?

Is it because we remember the world before the internet took over with a certain nostalgia. Is it the face of a rich pretty white girl who became the Snow White of victimhood. Or is it the underlying feeling that from the start we knew something wasn't quite right#, the story didn't make sense, the bigger picture was never able to fit in the frame? There are still so many unanswered questions. Do I think I know who did it, yes. Can it be proved, no. That's the difference between opinions and facts. It's only the facts that really matter in the end. The rest could almost be fiction. If this was an Agatha Christie novel all the characters would be gathered in the train carriage, and the protagonist would finally put the two theories to you the reader:

The first is that an intruder comes through the snow on Christmas night. They get in through a broken window in the basement with intent to kidnap a child. Things go to plan until they try to escape. For whatever reason they end up killing the child and leaving her in a locked room. Whether by luck or design they leave no fingerprints, no identifiable DNA, no handwriting that is recognised by anyone, and they never ever tell a living soul about what they have done. Keep this scenario in mind until after I have given you the next theory.

A wealthy family come home from a Christmas party. Its late. The children are tired but don't want to go to bed. The youngest child accidentally receives a series of injuries. By the time the parents realise what's happened she has severe brain damage and is most likely going to die. There is blood and signs of trauma around her vagina. If she goes to hospital the police will be called and people could be arrested. But it will not save the child. Having been through so much suffering in the last few years, the parents have a greater understanding of death than others. And so, a decision is made to cover up an accident with a narrative that looks like a real crime. They have a broken window, a maid desperate for money who mentioned a kidnap, the story of a man whose daughter was abducted many years ago, a father linked to a multi-national military company. To cover up the vaginal trauma the body is washed. To cover up the head injury and marks on the neck a garotte was created. To cover up someone in the family being involved a ransom note was written. Everything that happened to JonBenét would be put down to a stranger whom they know would never be caught because they don't exist.

And in a novel the detective would explain how they almost got away with it; if only they had cleaned away the clothing fibres, if only the police hadn't taken the notepad that morning, if only the phone had been hung up properly. In the final scenes the train would break through the snow and the truth would be revealed. But this is real life. There is only silence.

But how do the people involved ever move on from something like this? Surely is it there when they wake up, in those quiet moments during the day, and again just before they go to sleep. Does their conscience not haunt them in their dreams? Is there no redemption in the confession anymore? And when someone commits a crime, how long does it take for them to feel safe? You may be worried in the moments after, or the hours and days when you imagine someone has witnessed your transgression and is on their way to identify you. As time goes on you wonder if the police will make that knock on the door, and when they never do after six years, does it mean you have finally escaped justice? We go back to the main character Raskolnikov in the novel *Crime and punishment,* by Fyodor Dostoyevsky. A man who believes in killing an old money lender he did something bad for the greater good, and that his beliefs should not be bound by the same laws as those ordinary men leading lives of quiet desperation. He is beyond religion and politics. But for some inexplicable reason he finds that his soul cannot rest. In the end Raskolnikov confesses to the crime to clear his soul. What of those involved in JonBenet's death. How do they deal with a guilty conscience?

Perhaps the answer is in the final question: When is a crime not a crime? When it is an accident disguised to look like one. And if there is no crime then there is no question of innocence or guilt. The law has definitions of what is a crime and what is not. There are legal guidelines, stated cases, and a justice system designed to deal with the offences brought before them. But what if the reason we have never been able to solve this crime is because those involved believe there wasn't one? There was no kidnap, no sexual assault, no one strangled her, and no one intended to do her any serious harm. It looks as if there is, but it's all part of a pageant. One person looking at the crime scenes can say that an intruder committed a crime, but never find the answer; and another person looking at the same crime scenes can say someone in the family committed the crime and not find the answer. Maybe the truth is because there wasn't a crime.

It would also explain why the Ramseys have protested their innocence for all these years. You can ask them if they committed the crime, and they could honestly reply that they haven't because there wasn't one. Although this is strictly not true in the eyes of the law. The Grand Jury were probably right to go with hindering a police investigation. It is an offence, and Patsy Ramsey was guilty of committing this. The reason why she did so, we may never know. Perhaps she felt it was better to do a little wrong to help a greater good. How many of us would take the slings and arrows of public opinion to protect those we love? Let the people think a brutal crime occurred when you know the truth. Let them say that you might be guilty of a terrible thing when you know the truth. Let the media accuse you of being a liar when you know the truth. But there is a caveat to this: the truth still needs to come out. I think John and Patsy Ramsey were good people, but they had lost faith with the justice system.

Perhaps the great American tragedy is not that the country is now unable to administer justice, it's that it's forgotten the quality of mercy. Today politicians look away when good people are demonised because the mob deems it so. Lives are cancelled because a comment or act from the past has suddenly become a thought crime. But perhaps somewhere in the JonBenét investigation is the idea that the American dream is not dead, its merely sleeping. When we look at the two options of either an evil stranger has committed a terrible crime and evaded justice for years; or a normal family have covered up a terrible accident because they didn't believe they would get justice, I can sort of see the bigger picture and hope the second one is correct. There is a part of me that doesn't want this case to be solved with an arrest, trial, and conviction. Who would it help? Many lives have already been affected by the death of JonBenét Ramsey, and nothing is ever going to bring her back. But I still want to know how all the little details fitted together. It's not about justice anymore. If the American Dream stands for anything, it should stand for the truth, no matter how we end up framing the consequences.

References

Books

Jonbenet, Inside the Ramsey Murder Investigation. Steve Thomas.

Perfect Murder, Perfect Town. Lawrence Schiller.

Who killed JonBenét Ramsey, Dr Cyril Wecht and Charles Bosworth jnr

Foreign Faction: Who Really Kidnapped JonBenet?, James Kolar.

The Craven Silence, Nick van der Leek

Youtube

True crime rocket science

Carmen sandiago

Unsolved no more

True crime oracle

The Ramsey Case

Podcasts

True Crime garage.

The Killing of JonBenet: The Final Suspects.

True Crime Brewery

Printed in Great Britain
by Amazon

35855191R00207